CW00499354

How to be Chic in the Summer

Living well, keeping your cool and dressing stylishly when it's warm outside

FIONA FERRIS

ISBN: 9798832597003
Imprint: Independently published

Other books by Fiona Ferris

Thirty Chic Days: *Practical inspiration for a beautiful life*

Thirty More Chic Days: *Creating an inspired mindset for a magical life*

Thirty Chic Days Vol. 3: *Nurturing a happy relationship, staying youthful, being your best self, and having a ton of fun at the same time*

Thirty Slim Days: *Create your slender and healthy life in a fun and enjoyable way*

Financially Chic: *Live a luxurious life on a budget, learn to love managing money, and grow your wealth*

How to be Chic in the Winter: *Living slim, happy and stylish during the cold season*

A Chic and Simple Christmas: *Celebrate the holiday season with ease and grace*

The Original 30 Chic Days Blog Series: *Be inspired by the online series that started it all*

30 Chic Days at Home: *Self-care tips for when you have to stay at home, or any other time when life is challenging*

The Chic Author: *Create your dream career and lifestyle, writing and self-publishing non-fiction books*

The Chic Closet: *Inspired ideas to develop your personal style, fall in love with your wardrobe, and bring back the joy in dressing yourself*

The Peaceful Life: *Slowing down, choosing happiness, nurturing your feminine self, and finding sanctuary in your home*

100 Ways *to Live a Luxurious Life on a Budget*

Loving Your Epic Small Life: *Thriving in your own style, being happy at home, and the art of exquisite self-care*

Contents

Dear lovely reader,

Are you more a winter person than a summer person? Do you find it far easier to live in the cooler months where you can rug up in stylish layers and have that ski glamour look of loose tumbling hair and strategic bronzing powder on the tip of your nose and top of your cheekbones?

For some of us it's easier to be chic in the winter, and summer can be a real test of our patience. It's hot, maybe humid too, and we don't necessarily want to show off too much skin while we're trying to keep cool.

In our mind, perhaps from childhood, summer is a magical time of play and relaxation, but grown-up summers can feel far from that. We want to have a good time yes, but we also have to keep productive and look professional too.

In this book I share my favourite ways to be chic in the summer. All areas are covered – ideas for dining with ease, how to feel stylish in an effortless, carefree way, how to keep your cool physically and emotionally, and simple mindset switches which will help you languidly blow through the hot season like a cool sea breeze. I promise, with the tips in this book you will have your best summer yet!

Some of these ideas may not be new to you, but I hope many are.

There is no reason you must endure another summer ill-prepared. Read on to discover how you can create your most wonderful summer to date. It's going to be such fun!

Fiona

Chapter 1.
A serene diva mindset

So summer's not your favourite season. It's too hot and humid. You get all sweaty and uncomfortable. What are you going to do about it though? Hibernate in a refrigerated unit until autumn with a good book? (Actually that idea doesn't sound so bad...)

No, hibernation isn't an option, so your next best bet is to decide that **this is going to be *the* most fabulous summer**. Your best yet! You are going to float through summer like a diva – just picture her in a long, silky caftan, big movie-star sunglasses and hair pinned up in a chignon. And she's holding an icy drink too of course.

Let the diva lead the way. Let her show you how you can completely change your experience of the hot season by *changing your mind*. Have you ever noticed when something is bothering you, say a sore knee or a headache, and you keep complaining to yourself about it that it just gets worse? Then, you might get busy, someone calls you or you become engrossed in a task *and forget all about it*. It's as if it's not a bother anymore.

That's how I deal with the heat. When I turn my attention away from how hot and sticky it is and how wretched I feel, I don't notice it so much. Doing this along with practical actions is the key, and it's what this book is all about. But in starting with the mind and getting her on board, you will find it far easier for the ideas to flow.

It's as if we are unlocking the door to inspired action when we turn the key in our mind. When we drop the resistance to just how hot it is and how it *shouldn't be so uncomfortable*, we are open to new ideas and almost look forward to the rest of summer to put those ideas into practice. That's how I want you to feel!

Plan your serene and cool summer

Any achievement starts with a committed intention, and the summer of your dreams is no different. Decide for yourself that you are going to *create the best summer season you've ever had*. You are going to read through the tips in this book, research ideas of your own, and record the findings in your 'Chic Summer' journal.

You don't have one of those? Oh gosh, you'd better find one. You might have a pretty journal at home (you want one that is quite small, not a giant office notebook), or perhaps go shopping for an inexpensive pretty journal. And of course, if you are a high-tech girl, start a document on your computer or Notes page on your phone.

For me though, I like to have a tiny notebook dedicated to a topic, and pour out all my goodness there: a small lined notebook, the type that has a soft cover and stapled spine, and isn't too bulky. You can slip a notebook like this in your bag to take with you and write down ideas as you get them.

On the first page write '(Your name)'s Chic Summer' and say to yourself, 'This is going to be good! I am creating my best summer yet!'

Keep your ideas, dreams, wishes, desires and plans in your secret garden and let them be just for you. Don't even share them with your husband or your children or whoever is closest to you. Resist the urge even though you are excited and want to share your inspiration!

I am saying this from experience. Sometimes my bubbling enthusiasm was well received and sometimes... it was not. All I got was a bemused, confused look and I felt my happy, sparky energy dilute. It just seems to be something that happens when you let it out. You need to harness your enthusiasm and have it power you rather than let it out to spill all over the place. It is no good to you there!

Claim success for yourself

Now that we've got that sorted, let's move on – to you, being awesome, all through summer!

You get to have the summer of your dreams
You get to enjoy yourself
You get to be chic and serene
You get to quantum leap ahead in your mindset
You get to rise above the reality of day-to-day life
You get to create an inspiring summer wardrobe
You get to live in a state of ease and peace

It really is as simple as deciding; I've proven it to myself time after time. When I moan and complain about how sweaty I am, how my top is sticking to my back and how my hair has gone all floofy around the bottom yet strangely flat on the top, my creativity is cordoned off. I have nothing to go on with.

But when I look the other way in my mind, towards what I would rather experience, suddenly I feel better; more inspired and hopeful. 'Where there is hope there is movement' is a phrase I heard someone say once and it's so true.

We get to create our own experience and it all comes from a calm and optimistic state of mind. We really are so lucky in that we get to create any experience we desire. It's up to us! And we can choose anything we like. Don't get stuck in complaint mode, start creating instead. It's so fun, you will be thrilled with the results, and the best thing of all, life just gets better and better.

Your Chic Summer tips:

- **Plan for a chic summer**. Decide how you want it to be and then decide for yourself that it will happen.

- **Be excited for a wonderful season** to come and know you will love it. Make the intention that this will be your best summer yet, because you decided it would be. It's that simple.

- **Don't tell anyone your plans**! Keep them as your own secret energy source and let your exciting thoughts and dreams power you from within. This really is a crucial step, I can't stress it enough!

Chapter 2.

Your 'fabulous summer' plans

Part of being intentional in creating a brilliant summer is to actually do all the things you always say you want to do. It sounds so rudimentary but an important missing step for me was often the doing! Perhaps you too? You have a wonderful glimmery perfect vision of how your summer is going to look, and then when the leaves start falling you look back and think, 'Where did summer go? I never did those things... Oh well, next year'.

And is next year any different? Of course it's not! I know this pattern *so well*, but you know what? This summer *is* going to be different. It really is! This summer we will do all the 'things we always thought we'd do in summer', such as:

- Making a picnic of gourmet goodies and going to a lovely park (we have had our picnic basket set for over ten years and it's virtually brand new).

- Swimming at the beach (we live near two lovely beaches and never go).

- Playing mini-golf (we did it once with friends who stayed and it was a lot of fun).

- Going to a farmers market (I never get organized early enough and when I am ready to go they're finished for the day).

- Being a tourist in your own town and seeing the sights (people come from all over the world to see 'Napier, the art deco jewel' and living here we take the beautiful architecture for granted).

These are all outings my husband and I would make an effort to do when guests stayed, but rarely for just the two of us.

And then there are the things we have already started doing, so we'll include those on our 'ideal summer' inspirational list too:

- Going wine tasting at local vineyards.

- Booking a lunch date and eating at a nice place.

- Dressing well and going out for a coffee and a window shop.

- Taking the dogs for a walk around the local park instead of down the road at home.

Make your own list and join my vow that *this summer* you are going to do at least a few of those outings, if not all of them! Even if the picnic happens on your own lawn. We did this last summer and it was actually really fun and felt different to eating at the outdoor table – more relaxing and vacation-like. It feels good to do different things even if it's a little more effort.

Here are some other enjoyable summer pastimes which will help you feel differently about the summer season. Remember, when you do things outside of your norm, it helps you feel fresh and new. I constantly amaze myself over and over with this 'revolutionary' concept!

Go to an outdoor movie. If you have these in your town, great! If not, no matter. Simply take your tablet outside and set it up. My husband Paul and I did this quite a lot last summer and it was so fun to watch a movie outside after dinner. We stood the tablet up on our outdoor table, set the sound to come through a Bluetooth speaker (for that surround sound movie experience), and sat outside in the balmy evening air enjoying our movie night with a glass of wine. It really feels like you've been somewhere when you change your setting!

Make a book list of summer titles to read. There is something so fun about entering the summer season with a stack of new books to look forward to. So they might not be new, and you might not have a stack, but you can still make a list to go through. Borrow books from the library (in print or digital), browse Amazon Kindle titles, or buy second-hand from charity shops if you don't want to purchase at full retail.

Choose titles set in glamorous, summery locations, or non-fiction titles which inspire you to be your best. Don't worry about the current literary darling, read what makes *you* happy. I love trashy novels and I don't even care that some may judge me for that!

Invite guests around. There are so many different entertaining options such as a barbeque dinner, drinks and nibbles, brunch or casual lunch. I always make the plans then figure out the menu afterwards. Inviting people around sets me off in a new, activated direction.

I tidy and clean the house more than I normally would. I create pretty touches such as cutting roses from our garden and creating a beautiful rose-bowl display in a big round vase I was given for a gift but rarely use. I choose a playlist to set the mood. I research recipes for sides or snacks. And then there is the good feeling that comes from seeing friends and family enjoying themselves, chatting away and relaxing. That feeling never grows old as I think to myself, 'I created this convivial atmosphere'.

Go on a walking tour. I love watching YouTube walking tour videos on our television; they make fun background wallpaper with good music when my husband and I chat with a drink after he gets home from work. But why not go on our own walking tour? In the area where we live?

Yes, it's just walking around your own town, but done with a plan and intention it feels different. You would map out a route, plan to walk past certain special points of interest, and basically go as if you were showing around a guest staying with you.

Or the advanced version, booking in with a tour company – wouldn't that be crazy? When the host asks where you came from you could say, 'Here!'

Be a summer gardener. I am not a proper gardener and don't have a vegetable garden, but I love planting tomatoes, cucumber, and fresh herbs in the summer. One tomato plant that cost me $2 kept us in tomatoes all summer, and same with the cucumber plant, except that was only $1!

I grow herbs year-round not just in summer, but there is nothing better to say than, 'I grew the salad myself', when you serve up diced tomato and cucumber dressed with olive oil, red wine vinegar, salt and pepper, and garnished with fresh chopped curly parsley!

Let yourself think of all the ways big and small that you would love to experience your ideal summer. Take inspiration from what you might do on vacation at a resort. You might lie by the pool on a lounger there, but at home, even without a pool, could you sit outside with a big floppy hat on and feel the sun on your legs?

I know it's not as easy to do this at home when there are always jobs to do that distract you from relaxing, but that's why this summer is different, you are going to sunbathe for fifteen minutes every day, just like you always imagined you would!

Your Chic Summer tips:

- **Be a girl who makes things happen**. Don't be like other people who always say, 'I meant to, but I just never got around to it'. You are not that person! You are someone who decides, makes plans, and then enjoys participating in them. You love your life. You have fun!

- **Research activities** in magazines, pick up ideas from books, and search online. Create a long, ongoing list of ideas that catch your fancy and occasionally, choose something to indulge in.

- Hold that **idealistic vision of the luxurious you**, looking glamorous and doing all those iconic summer activities. You, walking down the beach barefoot in a flowing caftan. You, laughing outside with friends on a warm evening. You, licking an ice cream with all the tourists admiring your town. Be your own cliché! It's so fun!

Chapter 3.

Chic motivation in the summer

When it's hot, and especially when it's hot and humid, *productivity goes down*. For all of us. It's hard to be inspired to do anything! Last summer we had an unusual anti-cyclone come down to New Zealand from the Pacific Islands and as a result had near 100% humidity along with high temperatures for at least two weeks.

I have a small air conditioning unit in my office which isn't often used, so I switched that on while I wrote, and when I was driving somewhere in my air-conditioned car I felt human again too, but we don't have central air in our house, and outside can't be helped either. This weather system really gave me a new appreciation for those of you who live in a humid environment. But we still do get it very warm where I live, sometimes over 30 deg C (late 80s F) and for days in a row too.

In the summer, when it can often be too warm to do anything after 8am, here are my best saviours to get what you need to get done and survive the day too.

Do your jobs early in the day

Even in the winter I always find I have more energy before lunch, and *especially* in the summer when the temperature rises as the day progresses. So I always try to get my hardest jobs done early. It really makes a difference to how productive I feel when I do this versus procrastinate all day. Of course it does! Procrastinating is helpful to no-one!

When I stop listening to my complaining inner monologue and just get moving to do everything as early as possible, I get the same amount done as if I'd spread my jobs out during the day but it feels *so* different. If you are someone who puts things off too, give yourself a push to do those tasks as early as you can, even if it feels silly preparing your dinner ingredients at breakfast time. I promise you will feel like you are on vacation later in the afternoon when you use this technique.

Make things easy on yourself

In the deep heat of summer, stop thinking you are being lazy when you choose to do as little as possible. *It is necessary for your sanity*. Simplify your life to the extreme, even if only for a short time while the hottest part passes. There will be time to do more in the autumn when your *oomph* returns along with the cooler temperatures.

If you are reading this book with enough time, it would even be a wise decision to plan ahead for a simple summer. Declutter a little in the spring. Hey, maybe that's why 'spring cleaning' is a thing? I know it's to throw open your home after a closed-in winter and air the place, giving it a good going over at the same time, but imagine using this process to prepare for an enjoyable summer too.

Along with decluttering, look at your social schedule and resist the temptation to sign up for new things over the summer. *No, Fiona, that bootcamp course is not a good idea. You will hate it half-way through and quit, having wasted your money and resenting that you had to go at all.*

Keep your diary open and easy with time to play, rest, go to the beach, or read a book in the garden. Personally I prefer to read a book inside, but I always have this dreamy vision of me on a sun lounger under a tree or umbrella, big sunglasses on, reading the latest airport novel.

Really look at what you have committed to in the past and practice zero-based thinking for *everything*. I heard about zero-based thinking from Brian Tracy many years ago, and he says to ask yourself, 'Knowing what I know now, would I get involved in this again if I wasn't already?' If the answer is 'No', get out of it as fast as you can. He says all this in such a calm voice that it always makes me laugh.

But it's true! If you have signed up for something that no longer suits you, or wasn't what you imagined it would be like, back out. You are not being flaky, it's called living your life the best way you know how. It's about learning from your mistakes. And really, they aren't mistakes, you are just finding out your *preferences*.

Some of us, me included, have erroneously thought that we must do as much as we can in order to live a full life. Well I now propose the opposite. Don't load yourself up, let yourself empty out. Practice natural attrition. Let things fall away. Feel a sense of peace wash over you. And if some things cling onto you like a limpet, peel them off!

Keep up to date with everything

As tempting as it is to put things off until it's cooler, you are feeling less sticky, more motivated and ready to tackle your jobs, *don't do it*. Keep on moving. Cross a few more items off your to-do list. Do a load of laundry once a day so it doesn't pile up. Don't wait until you're out of groceries to do a shop or your car is almost out of fuel to fill up. Pick up out of place items and put them away. Clear the kitchen counter and do all the dishes. When you notice something small, right it immediately.

Feeling hot and sweaty is draining enough without adding the weight of undone tasks to your load. Give yourself the gift of being on top of things and see how this helps you feel cool emotionally, which amazingly keeps you feeling 'cooler' physically. It's all too easy to blow your top at the worst moment when you are feeling overwhelmed.

It's far better for your mental wellbeing when you are efficient and productive, even if it's the last thing you feel like being. Sometimes it really is just a matter of putting one foot in front of the other and completing those tasks.

Play and relax

Having something to look forward to helps you feel more motivated to do your work too. It can also help you work faster and more effectively. You will move faster and won't waste time dithering. You'll want to get your jobs done so you can do something more fun.

And actually, when you have cleared your desk at work or tidied and organized the main areas of your home, this in itself is a reward. There is such satisfaction to be gained from gazing at a list with everything crossed off, or to come back into a room that has been tidied and fluffed up.

In my mid-afternoon slump time there is nothing to move me into motion again than the promise of a cup of tea and half-an-hour with a book at, say, 4pm. And, the trick is, to adhere to your promise – make sure you take that break. I know for myself I've said this, and then breezed through right up until the time my husband comes home, then I'm resentful that I haven't had any downtime. But I was denying it of myself! I know it makes no sense and that's why I try not to do that anymore. If you wouldn't break promises to someone else, why would you do it to yourself?

The main focus of this chapter is to simplify your life so that being organized and motivated is easier. Let yourself live a light and easy life by not having too much to care for. Every new item we bring into our home requires attention and management, whether it is a pet or a new cosmetic product.

When times are easy we don't notice the inventory building up, it's only when we are 'over it' and have 'had it up to here' with the relentless summer heat that we want to throw everything out and live a spartan life. I know I feel like that when my closet is disorganized and I can't find anything to wear and I just want to put something on and cool down already. You know, those days when you're already sweaty and you've only just started your day!

Be organized, keep your cool, let things be easy.

Your Chic Summer tips:

- Decide that you are now going to be **the kind of person who is effortlessly organized**. It really is as simple as making a decision! About anything! Yes, you are the girl who leaves work at a reasonable hour of the day with a clean desk. You get home to a fridge lightly stocked with easy meal options that are ready to cook. You have a closet which only contains clothing that you feel good in, fits you well right now, and is appropriate for the current season. Brainstorm just how it would feel to be like this, and note down little steps you can take to make it your new reality.

- **Commit to living a lazy life**, if not year-round, at least for the hot season. Consider it your summer break. Clear the decks come spring and plan for an easy three months where you do only the essentials as well as keeping everything else ticking over. Ask yourself how you can make your summer as *lazy* as possible.

- Keep at your trimmed-down to-do list and have tasks completed **as quickly as you can** so that you can enjoy playtime afterwards. Don't let your jobs spread to cover the whole day. Put your feet up! It's summertime!

Chapter 4.
On the best dressed list

These days there seems to be a competition to see who can dress the most casual: pyjamas out in public during the day, full-time active wear, leggings that leave nothing to the imagination, and beach clothes such as shorts and tee-shirts at nice restaurants. 'If it covers your body, you can wear it anywhere' is apparently the current dressing manifesto, and especially in the summer.

However, this gives us a golden opportunity to stand out from the crowd. With even the tiniest smidge of effort, we can look like we are on the best-dressed list, because everyone else is so casual. We can look like a movie star running errands in our flattering summer outfit and big sunglasses. We can channel a French Vogue fashionista with just a few strategic accessories!

Curate your summer inspiration

I like to keep my wardrobe and how I dress simple and easy, but sometimes this means I don't try new outfit ideas or styles. Going into a fresh season is a great time to look around at what's new in stores and online, just to keep current and not feel bored with our closet.

On Pinterest you can search specifically for your needs which refines what you will see. I know this is hardly revolutionary – 'how to search online' – *Gee Fiona, tell us something we don't know.* But I can forget so maybe you do too sometimes. A reminder is never a bad idea!

So, instead of searching for 'summer fashion', I'll try different terms such as:

Summer fashion over 50
Summer style mature woman
Summer fashion plus size over 50 (useful for flattering curvy girl ideas)

You get the idea. Searching for 'over 50' or 'mature woman' brings up classic styles for me to have a look at. I do also look at all ages too though, because it feels good to bring in elements of younger style to keep from feeling frumpy and old. Gosh it really is a balancing act isn't it!

I also like to look at celebrity style, television shows and movies, and even my favourite authors. You can search online for someone and include phrases like 'summer style', 'casual dress', or 'off duty style' after their name. Make sure to save or pin to Pinterest any you find, and see what kind of theme comes up over time.

Accessorizing when it's hot

The last thing I feel like doing when it's boiling is putting on the finishing touches. And sometimes I don't, I just do the bare minimum and go about my day. But most of the time I use little extras to feel like the fashion girl that I am.

Scarves are the classic fashion accessory, but we need to look for more creative – easier and cooler – ways to wear them in the summer. Instead of draping or knotting them around your neck, use them as a hair accessory. Fold a small-medium square scarf into a narrow ribbon and tie around your ponytail or bun. Use the same 'ribbon' to create a headband by knotting the ends together and using to push your hair back. Folded wider and used as a headscarf looks great too, very South of France.

Scarves also look stylish when you wrap one around your handbag handle so that it creates a handle cover, or simply knot it around one handle and let the ends hang loose. Or, on a day when it's not too hot to wear a top tucked into your jeans, choose a larger scarf, fold into a ribbon and use as a belt, threaded through your belt loops and knotted together where the buckle would normally be.

Necklaces can be bothersome in the summer because sometimes you just don't want anything sitting on your skin. When you feel like this, amp up your **earrings** instead. I usually wear plain 'diamond' or pearl studs, but I have a couple of pairs of longer earrings and will wear one of those. Being a bit 'extra' they take the place of a necklace and earrings.

A **cocktail ring** is a fun accessory to use too. I bought a set of four resin rings in pretty colours – yellows and pinks – and I love to wear one of these on my right ring finger in a shade that complements my outfit. They look more daytime and fashion-forward than a real cocktail ring made from metal and stone, even for those of us with a more classic style.

Inexpensive current season fashion accessories are a fun way to perk up your look. You can shop at younger stores and mix them in with your current outfits. This means you won't look too young *or* too staid. Just choose something here and there, no need to go nuts. And if something looks obviously cheap to you, stay away from it. The feeling you are going for is excitement, anticipation and in-love.

When you are a winter fashionista

Perhaps you love cool weather dressing more – the layering, the rich sumptuous colours and textures, and the general vibe of that crisp autumn excitement for a new fashion season. In this case, decipher why you love your winter wardrobe so much. Look at the outfits you wear, the shades you choose, and what silhouette you repeatedly graduate towards. Then, and this is the genius part, create a summer version of your winter 'uniform'.

Wear lighter versions of your favourite winter colours. Say you adore black, charcoal, white and plum in the winter. Your summer shades could be grey, dusty pink and white. Or you could use the same colours but choose summer styles in those shades. I always think someone in a black sundress with tan sandals and gold accessories looks so chic in the summer.

And there is the layering aspect too. Many of us layer our outfits in the winter, so how can we transition this style to summer? I have seen ladies who rock lightweight, gauzy layers, say a pair of cropped cigarette pants with a sleeveless shell top and a kimono style topper.

My winter version vs. summer version is as follows:

Winter:

Heavyweight mid-wash or dark-denim jeans
A camisole for warmth
Fine-knit wool jersey
Looped scarf
Ankle boots with a small heel and cozy merino socks

Summer:

Lightweight stretch jeans that finish just above the ankle in light-denim, bone, or white
Boho-style linen or cotton top with billowy sleeves that end mid-forearm, or a satin blouse, both either tucked in or untucked
Ballet flats or wedge heel sandals

(Or, a dress as an alternative)

Because I am such a jeans girl, I love to wear denim year-round.

Another angle to find new inspiration for your summer wardrobe is to look at the theme or style of your winter wardrobe – are you rock chick, Euro chic, or boho lady? Search for summer styles within that genre and see what comes up that you like.

If you are more of a winter dresser, perhaps you now have a few new ideas on how you can play with your winter 'uniform' to create a summer look you love just as much.

If you have put on weight over winter

Wait, isn't this the dilemma every summer? Well it is for me, or more likely, I planned to lose weight over winter and then... didn't. I'm exactly the same, or perhaps a little more. What if we all give ourselves a break and decide that the weight we are today is the *perfect weight for us right now*.

Personally, I am sick of always thinking I should be slimmer. It's a crazy silly waste of energy when you think about it. And if obsessing over it worked, wouldn't we all be skinny? But no, so let's try something new. Let's try focusing on our health instead. I know, I know, it sounds so boring. Dull. Worthy. But what I found when I focused on leading a healthy lifestyle, not slimness, was that I felt better straight away.

Instead of focusing on some far away goal weight, we can focus on today. Focus on how we can be healthy today. How we can adore ourselves and treat ourselves like a queen today. And the cool thing is that we can achieve this *immediately*, not when we weigh a certain amount. Talk about instant gratification!

I saved a great quote which always help me feel better about not being a skinny Minnie yet (because obviously I haven't tried hard enough, right?):

'By choosing healthy over skinny you are choosing self-love over self-judgement' (Steve Maraboli)

How awesome is that? Of course we want to love ourselves not judge ourselves. But by focusing on our weight, we certainly are judging ourselves. Whenever I get myself into a tizzy that I shouldn't be having treats and snacks, I come back to this quote, and I remember the self-love that comes with treating myself to a day of health. Beginning with thinking kind thoughts, calming my breathing, relaxing my muscles, and just. feeling. peaceful.

Find a dress that suits your figure

In the warmest parts of summer, dresses are a lifesaver. And once you find a style to suit your body type, you'll know what to look for in the future. The bonus of wearing a dress is that you don't have anything constricting around your torso to make you feel hotter than you already are, and it's so easy too; there is only one item to choose to put on.

There are 'dressier' dresses and more casual dresses available. For everyday wear I like lightweight denim, chambray or linen in a shift style, and the classic sundress style too – the kind that are semi-fitted around the torso and flare/pleat out to mid-calf. They are quite flattering to my shape.

If you find that your thighs rub with a dress, buy underwear that look like thin bike shorts. They're not tight like Spanx, they're just long-legged undies. These make such a difference, and there is no panty line either. You may also feel more secure wearing these than a pair of knickers under your dress.

It can take time to find your best dress cut, but once you do you're golden. And because dresses are such a seasonal item (you might only wear them three months of the year), they will last longer than clothing you wear more often. This means you can build up a pleasing collection of dresses by finding only a few a year.

Culottes are back!

As an adult, I have not found a pair of shorts that are flattering to my shape. And I feel frumpy in skirts, that's why I adopted dresses as my hottest-part-of-summer staple. But have you seen culottes making a comeback? Or perhaps they are always around, just under the radar. Culottes are a divided skirt, and that, often combined with fabulous side pockets, means they are a pleasure to wear.

They are like wearing wide-legged summer trousers, but breezier and quite feminine too. You can tuck in a tee-shirt or blouse, or do the French tuck where you just tuck the front part of your top in. If you manage to find any culottes, go and try them on. You just may find a new silhouette for your summer wardrobe. And they can be quite smart for office wear too.

Buy a pair of wedge sandals

If you don't already own a pair, do some research into purchasing a pair of summer sandals with a wedge heel. There will be a pair to suit your style. Some are chunky and younger, and some have a finer, more elegant look. They are easy to wear and will go with all your summer outfits from a floaty casual dress, to a dressier dress, and capri pants or jeans and a pretty top too.

I bought a casual pair with watermelon-red straps and a cork wedge at least five summers ago and have had so much wear from them. Mostly this style has a small platform at the front so you can be a little taller without wearing high heels. They just feel more glamorous than wearing flats, and if you choose some with a very mild slope then it can almost feel like you *are* wearing flats.

Backless sandals are very popular I have seen, but I just can't get excited about them. Maybe you have better luck, but they don't seem stable to me, and they also come across as a bit old fashioned, especially when paired with a heel. I much prefer my sandals to have a back strap or closed-in heel, but you may be different. You might love them!

Swimsuits

Out of all summer dressing, I think it's swimsuits that have us ladies quaking with horror the most. It really is the worst of our nightmares, is it not? Stripping off to our underwear and parading around in public? Because that's what it is like! I have a few thoughts on this...

Once upon a time I wore bikinis. I was slimmer than now but never skinny, and I wore them in my thirties and forties. I just didn't care what people thought, and I also only wore them on the beach or around the pool. Everyone else had swimsuits on too so it didn't matter. I certainly wasn't the type to wear cut-off jean shorts and a bikini top in a normal public environment!

Then one day they didn't feel so right anymore, and that day I went shopping for a one-piece swimsuit. I spent a little more than I normally would, to get a pair that had supportive cups and sucked in my mid-section. They are a simple style in a dark navy which is almost black. When I went shopping to choose them I went by myself and visited multiple stores. I chose a day when I felt good about myself, 'normal' if you will. I approached the whole exercise from a practical point of view, and also went as fast as I could. I was extremely efficient about the whole thing and that's what made it easier.

I walked into a store, went to my size, chose pairs I liked the look of and then had a big trying on session. I did *not* blame myself if the swimsuit looked terrible. It just meant it wasn't the right cut for me. It was the swimsuit that got the blame, not me. I also didn't criticize my thighs or any other part of me. Not that I didn't notice them, it was just a decision I made and it was very helpful.

When I found the most flattering pair I asked the sales assistant to put it aside for half an hour, then went to the next store. There were only three stores to go to; the city where I live isn't very big. And one store I didn't even try any on, because all the choices were very sporty, and I wanted a pretty, feminine swimsuit.

When I had exhausted my options, I went back to the store where the swimsuit was that I liked the most, quickly tried it on again to confirm, and bought it. Making this an entirely logical, practical exercise meant my emotional female brain didn't have time to freak out. I also had a deadline of meeting my niece for a swim the next day that meant I needed to choose. This was helpful! I made the best decision at the time, chose, and moved on with my life.

My recommendation for you is to work with or create a deadline. If I didn't have one I could have easily gone home empty-handed, over-thought things and dragged the whole situation out, and not with a better result either, because I love the pair I chose and still happily wear them today, two years after purchasing. Because I don't wear them often they have stayed new looking, and I chose a simple, classic style so it will be a long time before it dates.

A tan helps everything

One way I have found excellent to look better in all my clothes is to do a little self-tanning here and there throughout summer. I have only had a spray tan once, to go overseas on vacation, and I don't think there is the need for that expense on a regular basis. Well not for me anyway.

Keeping a bottle of gradual tanner in my bathroom cupboard keeps me looking lightly tanned without much cost or upkeep. (There are more details in *Chapter 7. Pretty and fresh summer beauty*).

Using gradual tanner on my legs, arms and decolletage, and bronzing powder on my face makes me look sun kissed without the sun. Even if you are wearing cropped pants you can put a little on your lower legs for your legs to look more tanned. Or a tiny amount on your forearms when wearing a top with sleeves. And when you wear something sleeveless, or shorter sleeves than normal such as cap sleeves, tanning lotion does wonders for the upper arm. Upper arms are never our favourite areas, are they! But tanning lotion helps enormously.

You'll think you will be the only one to notice, but I promise you that will not be the case. One day when I had put on a little more than usual, because my husband and I were going out for lunch and I wanted to have a bit more oomph than normal, he noticed. I had also applied a dark navy smoky eye with my look. He said, 'Wow, you look great! The tan,' (as he waved his hand at my arms and face) 'the eyes. Do that again'. Now, my husband often says I look nice, but never with this much enthusiasm. It was definitely out of the ordinary and I haven't forgotten the nice feeling!

The main thing that I have found most helpful for summer is not to be too self-conscious with what I look like. Lots of ladies are in the same boat, worrying about what to wear and how others view them. To put it plainly, most people are more concerned with themselves to worry about what *you* look like. My mother always said this when I was growing up and it's so true! And so relaxing when you feel like all eyes are on you.

My best encouragement is to put time and energy into putting together a summer wardrobe you are happy with, whether it's twelve pieces or a hundred pieces. Then, forget about it. Wear your clothes, enjoy them, but *enjoy what you do in them more*. Enjoy the people you have around you. Enjoy creating a fun summer and release yourself from self-judgement. It's just not worth it. Life is too short!

Your Chic Summer tips:

- Decide that you are going to **look towards the new summer fashion season with excitement** rather than dread. Perhaps you will take this opportunity to tweak your style direction or even try on a whole new persona. Keep your thoughts in your secret garden and just turn up looking fabulous. No need to tell everyone about your inspiration or that you are trying a new style.

- **Curate your ideal summer wardrobe and be ruthless with the rest**. Maybe you aren't brave enough to get rid of the cast-offs just yet, but at least give yourself space and permission to pare your closet down to your absolute favourites. You are a lady who no longer settles for mediocre. You are someone who is going places! Uphold your own personal standards when it comes to style. Throw out anything that hangs there quietly throwing off frumpy vibes. No one wants to age prematurely! And even when you are older you don't want to be 'old'. I went shopping for a few new nightgowns with my 78-year-old mother-in-law when she stayed with us recently. I showed her a few I thought she might like. Of one that was quite pretty with a large-scale floral print, she said, 'No, I don't think so, it's a bit 'grandma'', which I thought was so cute coming from an actual grandmother! Hearing this proved my belief that age has nothing to do with personal style.

- **Wear colours that make you feel happy**, whether they are cool neutrals, soft-brights like me, or shades of green, like my mother has done recently. She just found she was drawn to green and decided to roll with it. What are you being pulled towards? Follow the breadcrumbs and integrate a new shade or whole new colour palette into your wardrobe.

- **Learn to love self-tan**. Keep a bottle year-round and *use it up*. Don't just let it sit there going off (I'm speaking to myself here too!) The more you use it, the better you will get at application. You will learn from your mistakes and find out the best way to make it look natural and beautiful.

Chapter 5.

Your own personal stylist

Aah, a new season rolls around. It's fun to think of dressing yourself with a clean slate but then your mind screeches to a halt with all the limitations:

- Let's bring out last summer's clothes... some look appealing, some not so much.
- You remember that summer dressing isn't as fun as winter dressing.
- You've put on a little weight since last summer and have been able to hide this fact from yourself until now.
- You will have to show more skin – oh dear!

Let yourself have a mini freakout, then calm down, because guess what? Your personal stylist is on her way around. She is coming to your house and taking a look through your closet with you. She is going to help you curate a wonderfully simple, luscious and divinely inspired collection for you to look your absolute best this summer. It's exciting to think about!

You hear a knock on the door. She's here! You welcome her in and she envelops you in a fragrant, warm hug. 'Lead the way!', she says and follows you through to your bedroom. Together, you take everything out of your wardrobe and lay your clothes on the bed. She gets you to get all your shoes out too.

Firstly she asks you to put away all your winter clothes, either on hangers to the less accessible areas of your hanging closet space, or in drawers or containers. And the same with your winter shoes, she helps you pack them away neatly. Then she asks you to talk her through your warm weather options.

Specifically she asks:

- *Which of these clothes do you absolutely love and make you feel happy looking at them let alone wearing them?*

- *How do they make you feel? Is there a persona you feel is brought out when you have them on?*

- *What colours are your favourites out of all of your summer clothes?*

- *What colours make you feel drab or frumpy and not like yourself?*

Once you have gone through the clothes you already own, your stylist then starts brainstorming back and forth with you, asking:

- *If you looked like the ideal you of your dreams, with the perfect figure, amazing hair and ageless complexion, how would she dress? What outfit comes to mind for you?*

- *How does she feel in her clothes?*

- *Where does she shop since she has no financial limitations?*

- *How would she love to come across to others?*

- *Does she have any style favourites in movies, television programs, celebrities or people she knows in real life? Who are they and what does she love about their style?*

As you chit chat with your stylist and answer these questions for her, she sifts through your garments and also scribbles down a few notes in her spiral-bound notebook. At the end of your session, which, even though it was two hours long has flown by, you gaze in wonder at your 'new' closet.

It looks incredible. Your clothes, that were already there before she arrived, look brand new and so enticing. They are hung in colourful sections and there is a neat stack of donations by the door. You have a short list of items that you can't wait to go shopping for. You had such a fun time with her and suddenly dressing for summer doesn't seem so daunting. You even feel more confident in your body and comfortable in your own skin, despite not being as svelte and trim as you'd like.

Can I let you in on a little secret? The chic personal stylist? She is you. And she can come around to your place today if you like. Shall we make an appointment? All you need to do is have a quick tidy of your bedroom (make sure your bed is made before she arrives!), have a shower, dress in comfortable, tidy clothes, put a little makeup on (if you wear it), and style your hair. When my stylist comes over I like to put my hair in a loopy ponytail or fashionable high messy bun so I'm ready for action.

Then, go through the steps in this chapter with her and think about the questions she has presented you with. You can think of them in your head or write them down. Whatever suits you best.

I'm inspired to do this too, so let's go through my Q&As together and then you can get started on your own!

Okay Fiona, it's personal stylist Fifi here, can you answer these questions for me?

Which of these clothes do you absolutely love and make you feel happy looking at them let alone wearing them?

I love my soft, stretch skinny jeans in washed out blue, and the white pair too. I also love my colourful boho-style tops.

How do they make you feel? Is there a persona you feel is brought out when you have them on?

They make me feel cheerful and feminine when I wear them. It's a combination of the soft-bright colours and gathered billowy sleeves of my boho tops. When I wear these clothes I feel confident, alluring, eye-catching and relaxed. I feel well-dressed and like the next-level me, but also grounded in comfort.

What colours are your favourites out of all of your summer clothes?

The neutral bottom halves in soft washed-out shades, and the soft-bright top halves in candy pink, emerald green, sunshine yellow, soft red and bright navy.

What colours make you feel drab or frumpy and not like yourself?

Sage green, brown... they look so muddy on me.

That's great Fiona, let's move onto our next set of questions. These ones are so much fun to think about!

If you looked like the ideal you of your dreams, with the perfect figure, amazing hair and ageless complexion, how would she dress? What outfit comes to mind for you?

She would have smooth, lightly bronzed skin, hair worn loose and wavy or caught back in a low ponytail, and she would sashay in pretty summer dresses that are cool to wear and look wonderful on her.

How does she feel in her clothes?

Easy, relaxed, elegant, at peace.

Where does she shop since she has no financial limitations?

Mmm, Chanel perhaps? Can I bring a touch of Chanel style to my look without the Chanel budget?

How would she love to come across to others?

Effortlessly chic, situation-appropriate, enviable yet accessible.

Does she have any style favourites in movies, television programs, celebrities or people she knows in real life? Who are they and what does she love about their style?

- Estée Lauder's granddaughter Aerin Lauder – I love to view her casual styles to see how an elegant billionaire heiress dresses at the beach or out to lunch :) She was born the same year as me too which inspires me – she is my age and shows me what is possible.

- Character Georgina Clios in the Riviera streaming series – She is my dressing inspiration since where I live has a similar summer climate (most of the time) to the South of France. It can get very hot here. Georgina wears a lot of flowing colourful dresses and big hats. She is my dress-up inspiration.

- Sofia Vergara – It helps me to look for style role models with a similar physique to me, with Sofia it's a big bust. I'm not as slim as her but I do have a big cup size. It's not good for me to view model-types with a modest bosom as the clothes never look as good on me!

Now it's your turn. Are you up for a visit from your stylist? I promise you will have fun, and even though it's just 'you', you will come away with a renewed vision for your summer wardrobe, *and* a tidied closet with items you will happily want to wear as it gets warmer. Plus, a petite list of needs to start looking for.

Your Chic Summer tips:

- **Be your own stylist**! Go through this chapter as if it were you. Do a quick tidy of your house and make the bed, shower, dress and do your hair and makeup as if for a casual day at home. Put some soft instrumental music on (search BGM or background music on YouTube and play it through your phone). Then welcome your lady in – actually go down the hall and open the front door to her! – and together go through all the steps in this chapter.

- **Channel a favourite character**. Be a vintage persona like Catherine Banning from *The Thomas Crown Affair* movie, or Georgina Clios from *Riviera*. Take on their cool confidence as your own and borrow from their chic personal style. It really does help to amp up your own motivation! Find yourself a journal or even a note pad and jot down answers to your stylist's questions and also **ideas and inspirations** as they come up.

- Own your style and **be confident** with it. Any look is *immeasurably* improved with a dash of confidence worn like a jaunty silk scarf.

Chapter 6.

40 ways to dress chic in the heat

This is our biggest dilemma isn't it? How to look cool and casual, or polished and professional (depending on where we are), when it's boiling outside. When our makeup slides off our face just *thinking* about stepping out of the air-conditioning. And some of us don't even have air-conditioning!

In this chapter I share all my best tips to stay cool and be chic. Use some of them, use all of them, pick out the ones you like best, adapt them to suit. It's a pick'n'mix of inspiration for you to employ as you will and may even spark off ideas specific to you too. Note all yours down so you remember them when it's too hot to think.

1. **Wear your hair back** if it's longer than shoulder-length. I like a low or high ponytail, maybe with a small scarf tied around the elastic.

I have also seen some ladies clip their hair back at the sides with pretty clips, because not having hair flopping in your face can have you feeling less hot and flustered too.

2. **Choose fabrics that skim** you rather than cling. Natural fabrics are great, but even some manmade fabrics can be lovely and cool. Just choose fabrics that hang loosely.

3. **Wear tops untucked** or with the French tuck (just a tiny part of the top tucked in at the front). Even though I am definitely not skinny, I have been enjoying tucking tops in, but when it's hot there is nothing nicer than a bit of air getting up under your top. Choose tops that have a nicely shaped lower hem so it looks intentional!

4. If you like to cover your arms even in summer, **choose sleeves that are flowy** or billowy. As with an untucked top, air can get in to cool you, versus a fitted sleeve.

5. **Wear open-toed shoes**. You might want to paint your toenails, but open-toed shoes make such a big difference to how warm you get, and the bonus is that as you walk, airflow is encouraged. It's like air-con for your feet!

6. **Think 'loose'** when it comes to dressing. The looser the garment the cooler you will feel. I love

my skinny jeans, but in the summer I'll switch to wide-leg pants or lightweight boyfriend jeans.

7.   Find **dresses that suit your figure type** and start collecting a few each year. Build up your collection! Dresses really are the ultimate when it's hot, and they can be casual, dressy or corporate. There are so many styles, and yes, this means it can take a bit of time to find your ideal shapes, but once you do you'll know exactly what to look for.

8.   **Go for fabrics with some 'heft'**. You would think the opposite would be true, but very fine fabric can cling when you start to 'glow'. Of course you don't want fabric that is too heavy, so find the sweet spot when you are shopping for clothes.

9.   Take a **large feather-light scarf** that goes with your outfit. Keep it in your bag, but know it's there if you're in cold air-conditioning, or even if you are outside and can feel you are getting too much sun.

10. **Wear clothing that is unlined**. An unlined jacket is so much cooler to wear than a lined jacket, and will give a more summery look too.

11. **Wear light or mid-tone colours**. Darker colours can absorb heat or even just feel hotter. The look of colour really makes a difference! If a

colour is cool to look at it will produce a similar feeling when your wear it. Or you could just ignore that and be a glamorous vision in black!

12. Consider **wearing less jewellery**. Metal conducts heat which I realized when the buckles on my sandals started searing into my skin while we were tourists in Las Vegas a few years ago. On the hottest days minimize the jewellery you wear and keep earrings to studs, etc.

13. **Wear a floaty over-sized top** with slim leg pants. You can still feel like 'you', but cooler. For some of us with a bigger bust and perhaps not as slim a torso as we'd like, this look can be more flattering than the fitted top, loose pants combo (I wear both, but the loose top/fitted pants is my preferred outfit).

14. **Have a summer handbag** – raffia or basket type bags can look cute with a casual outfit, and less 'heavy' than a traditional handbag.

15. **Dampen a cotton scarf**. One particularly hot day I took a cotton square and dampened it, then twisted it into a rope and tied it around my neck. It didn't even look wet, and instantly cooled me down!

16. **Skip the sunglasses** sometimes. Sunglasses are great when it's glary, but sometimes they add to the heat for me, and worse, start sliding

down my nose making a mess of my makeup. At those times it is better to forgo sunglasses altogether.

17. **Think cooling thoughts**. When all that's on your mind is how hot it is, you can't concentrate on anything else, and I believe this makes you feel hotter. Instead, ignore the heat and think icy cool thoughts – actual icebergs in cold water if you need to – and get on with your day.

18. **Wear less makeup** than you normally would, and make sure to set your makeup with a little powder. Too much can look cakey, but a light dusting on your t-zone will look pretty, and preserve your look.

19. **Choose a visor** over a full hat. Not only will it not wreck your hair, but it's cooler than having your head covered. They don't need to be sporty, I have a pretty visor made from natural-coloured woven fibre.

20. I have not tried this myself, but so many ladies have told me they **keep a pretty fan in their bag**. And why not? They barely take up any room, and you would look quite elegant and 'regency' fanning yourself when it's warm.

21. Go through your bag and consider taking only the essentials with you. Carrying a big tote or even a chic backpack generates heat against

your body compared with a **smaller shoulder bag** or crossbody style.

22. Look at clothing which has **cut-outs or 'holes'** such as the 'cold shoulder' style or *broderie anglaise* type fabric. I have a pink blouse in this fabric and the little holes all over definitely help me keep cool, especially when I am walking along!

23. **Dress in layers** if your workplace has very cold air-conditioning. A loose shift dress with a lightweight jacket or cardigan is a classic solution. A more casual look is the t-shirt and large loose-weave scarf combo.

24. **Smooth your hair back** into a slicker style if you have high humidity. My hair instantly puffs into a frizz with moisture, so I spray a little hairspray on a brush to tidy my hair into a sleek ponytail on a humid day.

25. Wear **soft-bright and happy colours** for a zingy energy. You don't need to accessorize as much when you wear more colour either, which helps keep the heat factor down.

26. Take off all your jewellery when you come home and **change into cool and elegant loungewear**. I like wide-leg satin lounge pants and a tee-shirt in a feminine colour, and the only jewellery I wear is a pair of stud 'diamond'

earrings. I also tie my hair up into a bouncy ponytail or messy bun if I've worn it down that day. Instant cooling relaxation!

27. Wear an **embellished tunic over simple pants**. You will need little to no jewellery or accessories but still look polished.

28. **Use dry shampoo**. I am a new convert to dry shampoo! A little sprayed on the roots helps you feel better when hot weather leaves your scalp feeling oily, and it gives your hair a lift too – humid weather can flatten the roots.

29. **Try long-wearing makeup** such as Estée Lauder's DoubleWear. Ask for a sample before you buy it. I like to apply mine with a foundation brush so it's quite sheer, and not too heavy. I then go over areas again that need it. I still use powder because my skin is quite oily, but most people won't need to. DoubleWear really is different to other foundations.

30. When it's too hot for any jewellery at all, go for **a pair of statement earrings**. Make sure they are not too heavy, even if they're big. Some earrings are so weighty they will drag your earlobes down, which is not pretty *or* comfortable.

31. If you love jeans year-round like I do, **have summer jeans** and winter jeans. Summer

jeans are in lighter fabrics, perhaps soft and stretchy; and light colours such as washed-out blues, stone and white. Chambray fabric in a looser style is a great denim alternative too.

32. **Wear culottes** instead of a skirt. I never feel good in longer skirts, but I'm so happy in a pair of culottes! They feel 'safer' too with the divided leg. I never need to worry about an errant breeze or getting my skirt hooked up getting out of the car.

33. **Buy a strapless bra** so you can wear spaghetti strap or off-the-shoulder tops. Even larger busts can wear them, I can attest to that! I don't wear them all day every day though, just for special occasions when I want to wear a different top. It feels so summery and free to go strapless.

34. **Paint your toenails a bright, pretty colour**. Cool red or warm red are my favourites (I alternate). No matter what shoes you are wearing – even flip flops – you will look more polished, quite literally in this case. Nothing looks more summery than well-tended toes.

35. If you do choose a hat over a visor, **wear straw**. They look feminine and are cool to wear. Some even have no top on them for extra cooling ability.

36. To avoid hat hair, **wear your hat loosely** on your head rather than jamming it down, or tie your hair back in a low ponytail underneath.

37. **Wear cropped pants** for a little extra breeze around your ankles. Roll or tuck-under jeans or trousers for the same effect.

38. Choose a **new pair of colourful slides** for the summer. They are everywhere, and there are so many styles from high-end down to super-casual. A different pair of shoes changes the look of outfits you already own.

39. **Wear wedge-heeled sandals** in preference to closed-toe shoes. Cork heels are slightly dressier than rope or raffia covered heels.

40. When buying shoes **go for a fun colour** rather than neutral. They will make you feel cheery and summery, and you'll be surprised at how much they go with. I have a pair in soft watermelon pink/coral, and there is very little they can't be paired with in my wardrobe (and I don't just wear neutrals).

I hope you found at least a few new ideas to try in this chapter! Of course some of them you may do already, and others will be a good reminder.

Don't let summer beat you! You are that fashion-forward lady who sashays through summer with a serene smile on her face!

Your Chic Summer tips:

- As well as using the tips in this chapter, look around and **see how other people dress**. Take note of their shoes, their accessories and what colours catch your eye. Do research on Pinterest.

- Ask **people you admire how they keep cool** and still manage to look so good. Imagine if someone asked you that, it would be flattering, so don't be shy to ask others for their tips too.

Chapter 7.

Pretty and fresh summer beauty

We all want to feel polished and put together, and the heat of summer can make this a hard thing to achieve. In this chapter I share with you all my favourite ways to feel cool and fresh, and also to be ready for the horror of revealing skin that has been covered for months.

I know I can't be the only one who dreads getting their pasty legs out after a winter of cozy socks and jeans. It's almost like we've forgotten we even *have* legs. *Oh, there you are!* Don't worry, I've got you covered with all my best tips. I hope you find something new to try in this chapter!

Heat-proof makeup

I love taking the time to put on makeup each day, even if it is only five- or ten-minutes worth, however it can be challenging to apply in warm weather. I have found that it's helpful to let your skin cool down after your shower, and to let your facial SPF moisturizer soak in. So, do other things such as get dressed and have breakfast before you put any makeup on.

I always like to wear a foundation, and Estée Lauder's DoubleWear has been my favourite for many years. I like to apply it sparingly with a foundation brush so I can wear it quite sheerly and then go back to dab over any areas which need a little extra attention. Once my foundation has been smoothed on I apply a minimal amount of loose powder with a big brush. I tap most of it off and lightly dust all over. Too much foundation or powder can easily go cakey when it's hot, so apply the bare minimum of both and you will be pleased with the results.

Then, I apply my bronzing powder with another big brush. An Estée Lauder consultant taught me years ago to do the figure '3' on each side of my face, so go from the forehead/temple area to the cheekbone to the chin. I also dust a little down my nose. If I'm in a hurry I'll apply some to my eyelids with an eyeshadow brush instead of getting my actual eyeshadow out.

Then I comb my eyebrows (which I tint myself every month or so), apply more mascara than I think I need, and brush a tiny amount of dark eyeshadow along my lash lines with a tiny brush for 'eyeliner'. A neutral lipstick applied with a brush or from the tube and a dash of lip gloss on top and I am ready for my day.

With this makeup I feel polished and put together, but it doesn't look 'too much'. With well-defined eyes it doesn't matter if my lipstick isn't always topped up, although I do like the feel of moisturized lips. A light dusting of loose powder later in the day freshens up my look for the evening.

Try long-wearing makeup to see if you like it, and also how well it suits your skin. My skin is quite oily so I like it, but if yours is on the dry side it might be too drying. Some people love a tinted moisturizer in the summer, but for me it disappears and I look like I'm wearing nothing.

Do your research online and find new products to try. Most makeup counters will give you a sample of foundation so you can try it for a few days first and see it you like it enough to invest in (because foundations *are* investments, both in dollar cost and how long you will have them for, my bottle lasts six months at a guess.)

Protecting your skin from the sun

I am all about looking after my skin the best I can because we have to make it last our whole lives. But I do think sun protection has gone a little overboard. I am slightly suspect that skin cancer rates have increased along with the use of sunscreen. Could the chemicals in sunscreen along with the sun have combined to create some kind of reaction? I don't know and probably won't ever know, but it does make me happy to make my own rules up.

I think my main issue with sunscreen is that people put it on and then stay outside in the sun for hours. This has never appealed to me; when I was a teenager I never sunbaked because I ended up with a headache within a short time. I love the look of a tan but am not about to lay outside for hours.

The only areas I regularly use sun protection on are my face and decolletage, and this is because they both go pink if I don't. My arms and legs are fine with incidental sun and no sun protection, even in New Zealand which apparently is under an ozone hole. I did notice when we honeymooned in Hawaii that the sun was so much gentler there. I didn't apply sunscreen once on the whole trip and we were outside most of the day, between sight-seeing, swimming and walking to the shops. Whereas in New Zealand you can feel the bitey-ness of the sun on your skin very quickly. This is a signal to me to cover up or go inside rather than apply sunscreen.

I do think we all can use a little vitamin D from the sun, it feels unnatural to have no sun exposure. When my husband and I ran a retail shoe store for twelve years, my husband was told by his doctor at a checkup that he had low vitamin D and gave him some vitamin pills to take temporarily. My husband worked inside, went to the gym inside, drove a car home, and our home at that time wasn't conducive to outdoor living. I did all the same things as him except instead of the gym I walked outside most days for 30-60 minutes. That outdoor walking obviously gave me my vitamin D.

I see people being very black and white about the sun. Either they bake in it and look quite wrinkly and leathered... or they are slathered in thick white cream with a giant floppy hat and long sleeves. I have decided to be somewhere in between those two extremes. And I speak as someone who has had a melanoma removed!

You get to decide what is right for you. Be sensible but don't be paralyzed with fear by all the scaremongering in the press, that let's face it, is probably designed to sell you more products. A little common sense goes a long way when it comes to the sun.

Find a hairstyle you can wear 'wet'

One of the worst style *faux pas* is to leave your house with wet hair, but this is exactly what I am encouraging you to do when the weather is boiling. On the hottest days there is nothing more cooling than damp hair. The trick is to work out a hairstyle that looks polished and chic, not one that makes people think you woke up late and ran out the door straight after your shower.

My go-to is to comb a tiny amount of gel through towel-dried hair and make a part on the side. I then slick it back into a low ponytail and wrap this around and fasten into a bun with a few bobby pins. A small silk scarf folded into a long ribbon wrapped around the base of my bun and tied into a short knot finishes the look off.

If your hair is shorter but still able to be tied into a ponytail, do the same, just missing out the bun and scarf. There are pretty elastics such as wide black, covered in pearls, or even a wide gold ring (a bit like a napkin ring) which will elevate your look.

Comb your hair after a few hours and put it back into the same hairstyle. Your hair will feel so silky and will look nice too. Not only is the slicked back style cool to wear and healthy for your hair (no heat styling instruments), but it wears beautifully under a hat and you can avoid humidity frizz as well.

If you have short hair, scrunch mousse or gel through and leave it 'flicky'. Your hair will dry quite quickly when it's warm. Practice new hairstyles when you are at home for the day so you can see how they turn out!

Stay ready

It's no use arriving at summer having neglected your skin throughout the winter. It's easy enough to shave your legs or have them waxed, but not so easy to improve the condition of your skin if you haven't moisturized it for six months. Get into the habit of daily moisturizing as soon as you've toweled off after bathing and see how quickly your skin responds.

Over the years I have built this habit and now it is rare that I don't do a full body moisturization every morning. And even if I do have to skip a day because

I don't have the time, my skin is okay with that because the base level of moisture is high. When I am washing myself in the shower I can actually feel how smooth and silky my skin is, and it's all down to body lotion, every day.

It doesn't matter if it's summer right now and you wish you'd started sooner, begin your new regime *today*. You only have today! Yesterday is not an option!

Caring for your skin along with applying a light self-tanner means you will always be ready for your day. You will always be ready to wear bare legs with a dress or a pair of shorts. I love gradual tanner which is body lotion mixed with self-tanner. Gradual tanner gives you a much higher margin of error; it's almost fool-proof!

If you already have a bottle of normal self-tanner you could make your own by mixing equal amounts of self-tanner and body lotion together, or even ¾ body lotion and ¼ self-tanner. Shake well! Then, use it every day or every second day to build up a light tan. Just make sure you apply normal body lotion lightly to your heels, knees, wrists and elbows first. This is my secret strategy for lightly tanned legs and arms without fuss.

There are also bronze-tinted lotions that don't 'tan' you at all, they just give you temporary colour. These are quite rich in pigment, so for a subtle look I will, again, mix some in with my body lotion for a light sweep of colour. I am also careful about what clothes I wear if I do this – if I am wearing cropped white jeans, I don't put any on my legs that day. Instead, I'll rely on yesterday's gradual tanner application and put normal body lotion on when I wear my white jeans. It's worth having this little bit of admin to not get bronzing lotion on light-coloured clothes!

Even though I love the cool, crisp look of a white tee-shirt or buttoned blouse in the summer, I have given up on them completely. Because I wear SPF on my neck and decolletage daily year-round, the necks would go yellow very quickly and it was not washable, even with bleach. Even sending to the dry cleaner! Apparently it is a reaction between the fabric and the sunscreen ingredient.

Instead I choose light summery colours such as blush pink, soft buttery yellow, and other pretty colours that are not affected like white is. You will have similar lighter shades in colours that suit your complexion.

'Stay ready' is probably the main message in this chapter. I know what it's like when I conveniently forget all the things that make me feel good such as keeping up with my grooming and making it habitual, and then wondering why I am feeling overwhelmed and grumpy. It's because I've ignored everything and it's all falling to bits at the same time!

Make your chic summer regime an enjoyable habit and you'll get to enjoy the payoff both in looks, and feeling relaxed and happy because everything is taken care of.

Your Chic Summer tips:

- No matter the time of year, **start your daily body moisturizing habit** *today*. Make it luxurious and pampering, not a should-do. Begin with something small you can achieve in one minute or less daily. Perhaps it's your elbows. Or your lower legs. Whatever you choose, do it every day. As time goes on and you have established the habit, include other parts such as your thighs and feet. Before too long you will be doing everything like me.

- **Try a wet hairstyle** on a day you are at home. See how it goes. Maybe you will find a chic new look that will become your go-to for summer. Or do the opposite; perhaps you will blow-dry your hair when it is the coolest part of the day or on a Sunday and make it last for quite a few days with dry shampoo (I like to spray a little through my hair before bed rather than in the morning).

- **Commit to 'staying ready'.** Use the products you already have and be ready to put your best foot forward each day. Enjoy the process. Be that next-level girl who looks and feels fresh and breezy!

Chapter 8.

Become a smoothie girl

Set yourself up for a successful and productive day by choosing a breakfast which will keep you cool *and* is delicious and full of goodness. Please allow me to suggest my absolute favourite, *the smoothie*. Many years ago my mother bought me a NutriBullet for Christmas, against my wishes might I add, and I have been hooked ever since.

I thought they were a fad, and that you needed to chew your food. I am so happy to have been proven wrong because smoothies have changed my life. They add a lot of nutrition into a meal, they are quick to make, they are water-rich, and super-yum too.

You might like hot breakfasts in the cooler months, but a smoothie in the summer is *heaven*. Not only is there nothing more refreshing than an icy blended smoothie, but it is good for you and keeps you full until lunchtime too.

You can make them in a normal blender, but I would recommend getting yourself a proper smoothie maker – a NutriBullet like mine or something similar. They are not so expensive these days thankfully, and have a different blade set-up which means they can blend solid items such as nuts, seeds and ice.

Over the years I have perfected a simple recipe for my breakfast smoothie and keep the ingredients on hand so it's a no-brainer in the mornings.

In my smoothie cup I put:

- A handful of fresh spinach leaves (and I keep a back-up bag of frozen spinach in case we run out).
- A serving of seasonal fruit (perhaps half a cored apple and half a lime including the skin, or a handful of mixed berries from the freezer. I also peel and freeze bananas cut into quarters – one or two quarters added into a smoothie is delicious!)
- Two tablespoons of mixed seeds (I buy any seeds I can find, mix them in equal quantities in a jar and scoop from this).
- Two Brazil nuts.
- Six almonds.
- A scoop of vanilla protein powder
- A sprinkle of something nutritional (optional, currently I sprinkle over some turmeric and

cinnamon, the quantities are low so you can't really taste it but surely it is worth having?)
- Four to six ice cubes.
- Top up with water.
- And finally, my secret ingredient, a bloop of olive oil (perhaps a tablespoon if you were measuring).

Then, whizz for longer than you think necessary as this really whips up your smoothie into the most delicious-tasting cloud of goodness you could ever imagine. Even my husband loves them, and just think how much nutrition is in that cup!

How to start tomorrow

If you don't have a smoothie maker and don't want to just rush out and buy one, there is another fabulous breakfast that I started with pre-smoothie days, and still have occasionally. It is the breakfast fruit bowl. I call it my vacation breakfast, because it's what we have if we go away on holiday and want to make our own breakfast rather than go out.

It is:

- Freshly chopped fruit. Maybe a whole apple if you don't want to buy lots of different fruit or purchase a pack of mixed diced melon.

- A dollop of yoghurt, or a couple of dollops. Don't be shy! My favourite is thick, unsweetened Greek yoghurt.
- Then top with chopped almonds. Currently I have the 'deluxe version' – in a container I mixed sliced almonds, toasted coconut flakes and freshly shelled walnuts and sprinkle a couple of big spoonfuls over my yoghurt.

This breakfast is so nice to eat and really does feel like you are dining at a tropical resort. And the yoghurt and nuts will help keep you feeling full until lunchtime too.

For beginners

If you don't eat any fruit currently, I hear you. A long time ago, over a decade if not longer, I didn't eat fruit at all. I thought it was boring, worthy and unnecessary. I know, harsh words against a delicious and healthy food category! But deep down I knew it was good for me (isn't that the death knell to healthy eating?), so I decided that rather than try to overhaul my diet all at once, I would add a piece of fruit to whatever I was having for that meal.

My favourite breakfast back in the day was peanut butter on grainy toast, and a café latte. So, I'd have that, plus a washed, freshly sliced apple. If you aren't ready to give up your favourite breakfast, just add a piece of fruit. You can pre-slice it and keep in a little container in the fridge the night before if you don't have much time in the morning.

This won't jostle your mind too much with big changes, and a piece of fruit will refresh you when the day has already heated up even though it's still early.

There are so many benefits to adding fruit into your diet, both in big ways and small.

- Fruit is water-rich which means all your cells will be plumped up with lovely hydrating goodness.
- Different colours mean different vitamins; they are all amazing for you!
- They are a gift from Mother Nature – she made fruit sweet and delicious to encourage us to eat more.
- When you eat what is in season it's cheaper and you also get what you need at that time of year.
- It's not that expensive because you don't need much – start off with one or two pieces each day and buy small amounts often so it's nice and fresh. What used to put me off fruit was that I can't stand over-ripe fruit or bruises etc. So, I buy a few pieces at a time and keep it in the fridge so it stays nice.
- Your skin will take on a healthy glow as you eat more fruit. I have heard that more fresh produce

in your diet gives you a golden glow to your skin. Who doesn't want that! It sounds fabulous!

- You can feel smug at the supermarket when others have donuts in their cart, and you have fruit in yours. Ha-ha, this is tongue in cheek but not really! Feeling smug is a great incentive to eat healthier!

Be that vibrant and vivacious girl who's had her delicious, chilled breakfast and is now set up for a fabulous day. Start with a small change or go the whole hog and order a smoothie maker. You get to choose!

Your Chic Summer tips:

- **If you are dairy-free or vegan**, change out the protein powder or yoghurt for your preferred choice. I use whey protein but there is pea protein and many other options, and there are tons of yoghurt choices too. Coconut yoghurt is divine. And can you imagine how delicious coconut milk would be in a smoothie? Yum!

- **Set up your smoothie station**. I keep our fruit and spinach in the fridge (or freezer, for our backup spinach and frozen berries), and I have a small basket in the pantry with jars of nuts and seeds, plus our tub of protein powder next to that. In the morning our smoothie basket means that everything is in the one place, and I just need to grab that. My best tip is to mix all the seed types into one container and then you only have to get 'one' spoonful instead of dipping into each jar or packet.

- Don't try and make **your other half join your fruit or smoothie crusade**. You do you and they will follow if they are interested. It's the only way.

Chapter 9.

Be the salad queen

Many of us just cannot get excited about salads. Like fruit, I used to avoid them wherever possible. But I now know better and have been converted into *a salad lover*. Knowing how good they are for me, plus that they can be delicious, *and* they are cooling on a hot day means I now search out delicious looking recipes and *actually make them*.

There are so many different kinds of salad too: creamy coleslaw with homemade dressing and charred sweetcorn kernels, the perfect Greek salad, a delectable Waldorf salad and so many others.

But what really made me love salads more was selling them to myself like a slick and savvy marketer. I reframed them from being a 'healthy choice' and 'something I should eat' to the sexiest of foods that is the answer to my dreams. Love or hate the Kardashians, I think we can all agree that looking good is a big part of their job. Well, have you ever noticed that they are constantly munching on big takeout salads in just about every episode? They are not eating donuts, people, they're eating salads.

So, I said to myself, *I'll have what they're having* and made salads fun and luxurious for myself. And it worked! I love salad now, order them when I'm out and even look forward to making one at home. I'm a healthy and glamorous salad girl don't you know. Won't you join me?

Pre-make elegant salads

Something magical happens when you rinse, spin and tear lettuce, wash and finely slice bell pepper, and generally prep your favourite salad vegetables. They crisp nicely in the fridge, and if you have made salads complete with your preferred protein already included, you have a delicious, healthy and quick lunch to grab.

Add a splash each of olive oil and red or white wine vinegar and shake it all around, then sprinkle with salt and pepper. I often make two- or three-days' worth at a time and they keep well. I promise you will find salads *far* more appealing when you don't try to put them together at the last minute. When they are instantly available it's like you are at a health spa retreat and have just been served a gourmet lunch with zero effort.

Find salad inspiration when you dine out

You can search for salad recipes online, of course, but also take note of particularly good salads you have eaten at restaurants or cafes. Either note down the ingredients that made your tastebuds zing, whether it was walnuts roasted in olive oil and sprinkled with sea salt, or pumpkin seeds (pepitas) toasted in tamari sauce.

My mother came across a salad at a café and now looks forward to making it for herself every summer. It is rare that she doesn't have it in her fridge, and she enjoys it every week. It is comprised of diced watermelon (she likes to remove the seeds), a thinly sliced red onion (as much or as little as you like), feta cheese cut into small cubes (she prefers firm feta rather than crumbly feta), and torn or shredded mint leaves. There is no dressing required because it makes its own 'dressing' from the watermelon juice within an hour or two. It is so refreshing and delicious!

Or, if it is a classic 'named' salad, remember the name and make it for yourself. I had a favourite French bistro in Christchurch when I lived there in the 1990s called *Le Bon Bolli*. It is no longer there, but the memory of their *Salad a la Russe* lingers, which I found out was a high-end potato salad when I researched it. No wonder I enjoyed it! I particularly remember the blanched green beans making it extra-delicious.

And if you haven't noticed many inspiring salads out lately, look up fancy restaurant menus online and take inspiration from theirs. Imagine casually saying at the table, *Oh that's Wolfgang Puck's chopped salad*, when guests rave about your food or co-workers ask what you're having for lunch.

Find easy lunches that you enjoy

It's fun to make a fancy salad recipe, but for everyday ease I have a small list of summer lunch ideas. For those days when I have very little time or energy and it would be all too easy to eat something stodgy that I will regret later on. They have to be simple to make with not-too-expensive ingredients, and most crucially, I have to look forward to them!

When I took my lunch to work every day I would make a big salad with loads of crispy vegetables such as torn lettuce, thinly sliced cabbage, bell pepper, fresh sweetcorn cut off the cob, sprouts; whatever I saw that looked good at the grocery store. Add to that some protein (for me, cold roast chicken or two hard-boiled eggs), a little container of creamy salad dressing and perhaps a sprinkle of grated cheese or toasted seeds on top and I was so happy to see my lunch!

'Toppings' are my secret ingredient. When I tried to make my salads 'too healthy' they were not so appealing. So I added in a few indulgences and now can honestly say that I look forward to a salad for lunch.

Add a salad to dinner

Mostly I have my salads at lunchtime in the summer, that way, if I've had fruit with my breakfast and salad for lunch, I know that if dinner ends up being less than healthy, I have front-loaded my day with good nutrition. But if I have a few fresh ingredients in the fridge I am far more likely to at least add a side salad to dinner.

It's amazing how a salad goes with everything, and when it's served up you are more likely to eat it. I like to go with the power of ease and *path of least resistance* when it comes to dining well. If I quickly make that salad and put it in a little bowl by my meal, I will eat it because it's there. And, it refreshes the palette too.

Growing your own

Last summer I planted a tomato plant and a cucumber plant. Both produced well, amazingly enough, and there were many nights when we had a tomato and cucumber salad dressed in olive oil and red wine vinegar with a sprinkle of fresh parsley and salt and pepper.

Even if you don't have that much space you can grow a summer vegetable plant and some herbs. The few dollars I spent were more than recouped, and because I am not a natural born gardener I didn't mind the financial risk if the plants didn't thrive – it was low! Plus, your own plants are spray-free.

If you grow a tomato plant, just be sure to pluck the side-growing stalks so that a strong central stalk can form. I did not know this until it was too late so I had a sprawling monster tomato plant that couldn't be staked, but no matter, I simply draped the whole thing over an outdoor chair and it fruited away happily until the end of summer, when we got our chair back. This experience showed me that plants are very forgiving and you really have to try hard to do anything wrong!

When it comes to being a salad queen, first decide it for yourself and start including more salads with your meals *before you find out you love them*. I have found that the more you have of something the more you want it. It works equally well with junk food or with salad, so why not choose salad? Be that gorgeous, glowing healthy lady in the future vision of yourself and choose to become hooked on salads. You won't look back!

Your Chic Summer tips:

- **Use up what you have**. Sure, you can follow a recipe and that's great too, but if you have a random selection of celery stalks, a carrot, and half a green bell pepper in the fridge, wash the celery and bell pepper, peel the carrot, and chop or slice everything finely. Mix them all together to create your own *salade du jour*. If you only have white wine vinegar and the dressing recipe calls for red, just use white. Or if you desire a creamy dressing and only have mayo, combine a spoonful of mayonnaise with a splash of any kind of vinegar and mix the two together with your salad vegetables. *Et voila*, you have made your own coleslaw dressing. Start where you are with what you have and then add different options as you run out of your current pantry stash. Don't rush out and buy all new ingredients when you still have your salad training wheels on!

- Remember your **herbs for the luxe touch**. Good restaurants always finish their meals off with fresh herbs. Torn fresh basil, finely chopped parsley or leaves of coriander. Add that extra touch to your meals for both taste and goodness. You can buy a little pot inexpensively. Choose your favourite herb and start with that, and keep it watered and in the sun. My no. 1 favourite is curly parsley, and I love thyme for cooking with.

- **Keep extras to hand** for salad toppings – crumbled feta, toasted pumpkin and sunflower seeds, and chopped almonds roasted in olive oil and salt are all delicious. Something extra sprinkled on top of a salad makes it more enjoyable, and you more likely to be a newly self-proclaimed salad lover!

- **Sell yourself on salads**. Find an enchanting angle that motivates you and changes how you see salads. Perhaps you will be the mysterious, glamorous lady ordering a Caesar salad when everyone else is chowing down on burgers and chips. Or find images online of someone you admire dining on salad. Sometimes it is just one tiny silly little thing that flicks the switch for you.

- **Investigate recipes** and immerse yourself in the world of salads online. In fact, just writing about salads in this chapter really makes me want to up my salad game even more!

Chapter 10.
The cool kitchen

In the summer it's hard to get enthused about cooking because it's just so hot. We don't want to heat up our kitchen even more than it already is.

I still like a hot meal at night though, because even if it's baking outside, it just doesn't feel like 'dinner' to me if the entire dish is cold. So I came up with loads of ways to get a nice dinner on the table and keep cool at the same time.

You may already know some of these tips, but maybe there are a few that are new to you, or encourage a different way of doing things. At the very least I hope you get one fresh idea to try!

Use your slow-cooker in the summer

Slow-cookers are not just for winter meals. When I think about it, I probably use mine more in the hot months. A slow-cooker doesn't heat up the kitchen like an oven does, and you don't have to stand over a hot pan cooking at the end of the day. Research 'summer slow-cooker recipes' online and you will find a whole new world of deliciousness.

Some of my favourite summer meals made in the slow-cooker are:

- Meat sauce for a burrito bowl: mix ground beef with a can of tomatoes, a can of chili beans and either your own seasoning or a packet of Mexican spices. Serve with rice and salad.

- Chicken breast cooked in teriyaki sauce and pulled apart with two forks to pair with a crunchy coleslaw.

- Making a 'stir-fry' in the slow-cooker. I have a love-hate relationship with stir-fries. I love eating them and *used* to love making them; I lived on them as a single girl. But something changed for me. I would plan for a stir-fry that evening and even chop all the vegetables and meat ahead of time. But when 6pm rolled around I had lost all enthusiasm for cooking and opted for something easier (read: takeaway food) saying that we'd have the stir-fry 'tomorrow night'. My husband even called it the 'stir-fry curse' after it happened several times. I think it was all the admin right at the time I was hungriest and tiredst. So I came up with what I think is a genius solution. The Slow-Cooker Stir-Fry! I'd put the meat and sauce in a cold slow-cooker, turn it on Low in the morning, and later in the day add my washed, chopped-small vegetables. I'm telling you, it was delicious, and couldn't have been any better if I'd done it in a wok. All you need to do at dinner time is cook the rice (or cauliflower rice if you want to be low-carb).

- Pasta meals – as with my 'stir-fry', it's simple to put all your pasta sauce ingredients in the slow-cooker, then cook the actual pasta nearer dinner time. Or even combine the pasta later in the day to cook in the liquid too. It's easier to do this with short pasta such as penne or spirals. With fettucine or spaghetti I'd cook this separately in boiling water near serving up time.

With all my slow-cooker 'recipes' I either turn them on Low if it's in the morning, or High if I don't get around to putting everything together until mid-afternoon.

Send your food out to the barbeque

I know, just like Meryl Streep in *The Devil Wears Prada* saying dryly, 'Florals? For spring? Ground-breaking', you are thinking the same about barbeque cooking in summer. But barbeques aren't just for entertaining a big group or making burgers.

Every so often we get a *Hello Fresh* box and I have learned a delicious way to cook from them. Basically you add one of their sachets of seasoning and a drizzle of olive oil (I like a *decent* drizzle) to a big bowl. Mix them together than add your meat – whole chicken thigh fillets, thickly sliced chicken breast or beef strips – and toss to coat. Use tongs or a wooden spoon to help with this. You can easily do this right at the time of cooking or prepare it earlier in the day. While the food is barbequing, the coating caramelizes nicely and the result is delicious.

In our pantry we don't have a stash of *Hello Fresh* sachets, so I recreated my own seasonings using the herbs and spices I already had. I never write them down and each time is different, but it sure is satisfying to get use from our pantry ingredients. I usually end up with 1-2 tablespoons of *Hello Fiona* seasoning once I add together salt and pepper, dried herbs and a spice mix such as Moroccan seasoning. See what I did there with my name? Why not do the same with your name when you make up an inspired seasoning mix!

With our cooked meat I'll do some potato wedges in the oven, made with chopped fresh potatoes on oven paper sprayed with oil, and cooked in a hot oven turning once. Add some crunchy coleslaw and you will have happy people dining!

Sometimes I'll buy a bag of pre-sliced coleslaw and make my own dressing by stirring through a few big spoonfuls of mayonnaise and a splash of white vinegar (or whatever vinegar I have on hand, I even used balsamic vinegar once which added a lovely flavour) as also mentioned in *Chapter 9. Be the salad queen.*

Or if cabbages are a good price I will buy one of those and cut a chunk off to slice very finely, grate in some carrot and stir through chopped parsley. Finely chopped red bell pepper is a nice touch too. I keep the slaw mix 'dry' in the fridge and dress a bit each day until it's used up. Or, if I know we'll use it all within a few days I'll dress the lot. Mixing in torn lettuce leaves is a nice complement to slaw mix too – in that case I would make a vinaigrette of olive oil and wine vinegar.

New gadgets

Have you bought an air fryer yet? We did! I resisted them for a while because I don't like fads, but, as with the NutriBullet I am happy I bought one. It's basically like a small convection oven which heats up quicker and cooks your food faster. It's great for making your own fast food, but thankfully there are healthier options which are just as delicious.

One of my favourites is to coat fresh fish (cut into big pieces like a restaurant does) in crumbs, salt, pepper and lemon zest, and spray with oil. Three or four minutes each side in the air fryer and you have crispy on the outside, moist on the inside 'fried' fish. Chicken breast stays moist in the air fryer too.

A summer vegetable bake is delicious and easy to make. In a small open casserole dish toss in olive oil and herbs a mix of any vegetables you like – tomato, zucchini, carrots, bell peppers. Slice or dice into similar size chunks and make sure all pieces are evenly coated in the olive oil. Season with salt and pepper and air fry for ten minutes.

All of these things can be made in the oven too, so don't worry if you haven't got an air fryer. I am always a fan of using what you've got!

Your Chic Summer tips:

- **Try new ways of providing dinners**. I always find that mixing things up at dinner time gives me a new enthusiasm for the kitchen. I love to eat, definitely, but coming up with dinner night after night and making sure all the ingredients are actually in our house can get old fast. I *know* you'll know what I am talking about. My usual method is going to the supermarket and buying groceries for the week and cooking old favourites that don't require a recipe. So, when I wanted to shake it up, I tried different things: we went out for dinner more, I tried subscription meal kits such as *Hello Fresh*, and looked up recipes on the internet too. My main dinner option is still what we used to do, but it helped reignite enthusiasm for cooking dinner when I introduced the other three options as part-time-workers as well. They add new ideas and new energy.

- **Get excited about all the delicious meals you are going to enjoy** once you reignite your motivation by choosing easy and delicious recipes or meal ideas. As with my salad queen chapter, writing this chapter has made me excited about cooking dinner tonight, when usually I am *not* that excited about it. I sincerely hope it is the same for you *reading* this chapter!

- **Make your own seasoning mixes** or purchase ready-made blends and use them to coat foods with before you cook. This is what I realized the secret 'sauce' of the meal kits we were getting was – *everything is highly flavoured.* Sure it's not 100% healthy and you might not want that level of flavouring every night, but it's nice every once in a while. When I make my own I start with ¼ teaspoon salt, then add whatever I feel like; maybe it will be garlic powder, smoked paprika and dried thyme. Or salt, curry powder, onion powder and dried tomato flakes. It's fun to create a new flavour *and* use up whatever herbs and spices you have in your pantry.

- Get your husband **on board with the barbeque cooking**. Send him outside with his giant tools while you prep the rest of the meal. The bonus of this is that the cooking smell stays outside, and barbequed food is *always* extra delicious! The richness is a nice foil to a fresh salad, or steamed vegetables dressed in olive oil.

Chapter 11.
Dine like a chic lady

When it's hot in the summer, especially at the end of the day when the heat has built up, it's hard to feel chic and elegant. This is when it is especially helpful to remember your chic lady alter ego.

Keep her in mind and plan for a successful day; a day in which you feel good about yourself and have had a nice time. There are so many little details you can add into your day which will elevate the experience for you and your loved ones.

Set your table like a restaurant

You know how welcoming it is when you walk into a restaurant to see beautifully set tables *en masse*? White tablecloths and napkins, a knife and fork already there, and maybe a candle or bud vase. It is such an elegant vista and it instantly makes you feel uplifted and relaxed all at the same time.

Why not do the same in *your* home? Have the dining table always be set for dinner. You can even reset it straight away after you clean up from dinner the night before if you want to. I like to set mine during the day, then it reminds me at dinnertime that I am a chic lady who dines at the table rather than in front of the television!

When our table is already tidy and set, it's an easy option, rather than scrambling around when dinner is being served up. Or having a tray on the sofa being the default choice.

And, if you have an area to dine outside when it's warm, designate a big tray to hold everything on it ready to go. You might not want to set your outdoor table with placemats, a napkin and cutlery too much ahead of time, so a tray does the interim job of gathering everything.

Build a collection of table linens

Just as you change out your bedroom linens and living room pillow covers from winter to summer, and put away your throw rugs etc, consider your dining table too. Over the years I have collected lovely tablecloths, placemats and cloth dinner napkins, all from thrifty sources: sale tables at fancy department stores, remnants and off-cuts of fabric that I've cut and fringed or hemmed, and from discount stores too.

In the early days when I had only one set of six dinner napkins, whenever I'd see something I liked and that was a good price, I'd buy it. This means that now I have a good selection of nice napery to use on a daily basis, plus a few better sets for special dinners.

In the summer I like to start with a white tablecloth or stay with a bare table, depending on the mood I'm going for. Next I'll put down round coiled rush table mats, then a soft cotton blue and white striped napkin folded into a long rectangle and a knife and fork on top of that. The combination of the woven jute matting and blue and white is beachy and summery but also elegant.

It makes a nice change from heavier fabric and richer colour combos that I like to use when it's cold.

To me it felt like I'd really graduated into being a grown-up when I started collecting table linens! Maybe you don't feel like you're 'quite old enough yet' but I promise you, it's a lovely feeling to sit down at a dressed table, and if you have people around, they will appreciate it too. Even if it's just your family, it will feel different when you sit down to dinner.

Create a menu of refreshing beverages

We all like to keep hydrated in the summer, but perhaps like me, you were feeling a bit same-same about what you were drinking? I mean, I love drinking water, but when I'm dining like a chic lady, a basic glass of water isn't going to cut it. But neither do I want to just have wine or a mixed drink near me, because when it's hot, it's easy to keep sipping to quench my thirst.

So I gathered a small selection of beverages for myself that were alcohol-free but also elegant and grown-up. It was fun to research, and I also made sure I kept them on hand, and chilled.

These days there are many options of lightly flavoured sparkling waters. I like to buy both larger bottles and individual serve cans, that way I have the option of pouring a few drinks for my husband and me, or open a freshly fizzy can if I'm the only one drinking it.

A nice touch that I have done for a few years now, is to freeze slices or quarters of washed lemons and limes, and use these for ice cubes in my drink. If there are pips in them I'll scrape them out with a knife before freezing. It's so nice to open the freezer and get my little zip-lock bag of fruit chunks out, and drop a few into my glass. They keep my drink cool, and once the citrus thaws it creates a refreshing flavour. They look stylish bobbing around too!

I notice on some television shows, the characters drink their water from a stemmed wine glass. I do this with champagne flutes, but in the summer it doesn't last long. So a normal sized wine glass with sparkling water, pieces of lime and maybe some ice cubes too is refreshing to sip, elegant and feels a bit more special.

I often thought to myself that I do the finishing touches when I make a gin and tonic, for example, but not for non-alcoholic drinks. They were like the poor relation! When I realized this I changed it, and now put just as much effort into my sparkling water drinks.

Summer wine

I also found there is a more grown-up version of sparkling grape juice available too – non-alcoholic sparkling wine. It's not as sweet, and really tastes like sparkling wine. I like to serve this at lunchtime. It's enjoyable to sip a chilled wine, but I don't feel all floppy in the afternoon, which even one wine can do; it makes me sleepy and *not* productive at all.

I opened a bottle of non-alcoholic sparkling wine when a friend came around to have sushi with me one lunchtime, and she kept checking that it was definitely no alcohol, because it tasted so real. She was concerned because she had to drive home afterwards! She had me worried then, and I kept checking the bottle in case I'd brought a normal bottle of sparkling wine out, but no, it was definitely 0% alcohol.

Another way in which I like to use this wine, is for an in-between drink. You will have no doubt heard the advice to have a glass of water in between alcoholic drinks when you are at an event. Along the same lines I like to keep non-alcoholic wine at home for when I might want another drink but don't want more alcohol. I can pour a glass and happily sip away, but still feel good and somewhat healthy.

And if you have a couple of sparkling wine stoppers or Vacu Vin corks in the kitchen, you can seal the bottles up for tomorrow night too.

Your Chic Summer tips:

- Imagine you are **that chic lady in her fabulous home** in the country, at the beach, or even the South of France, and ask yourself, How would she dine? How would she set her table? And what would she have in her glass?

- **Set your table *tonight*.** Decide that you are going to be a lady who dines at a beautifully set table. You can have it be as simple as you like. If you are worried about napkins becoming stained, don't be. They are there to be used, not just sit in a drawer. If they are clean and it is for your family, refold them at the table at each person's setting. I put them in the wash if they are dirtied, or if we have a dinner party; then I throw them all in the wash. A normal warm wash along with your kitchen cloths and tea towels will clean them up (every so often I have to wash one twice but mostly they are fine the first time). I then fold them straight off the line or from the drier, no ironing necessary. Once they are in the drawer, put at the bottom of the stack so napkins are rotated evenly, the weight of the other napkins 'irons' them for you.

- Next time you are at the supermarket, buy a few bottles or cans of **flavoured sparkling water or non-alcoholic wine** to supplement your drinks stock at home. Keep everything in the fridge if possible so they are nice and icy cold when you want to pour a drink. When we moved to our current home, the kitchen had a built-in fridge, so we got to put our own fridge in the garage as a drinks fridge. It is such a nice extra to have if you ever get the chance. You might even find an inexpensive option. You can keep it colder than your normal fridge, and it's lovely to offer guests – or yourself! – a chilled beverage from your selection.

Chapter 12.
The summer home

Doesn't the phrase 'a summer home' sound so pretty? People who have a second home can talk about getting away to their summer home, country house, or little cottage by the lake. For those of us who 'only' have one residence, I thought it would be a delightful project to look at *our* home as a summer home. At just how our home that we see every day can be a vacation home or weekend getaway for ourselves.

In *Chapter 2. Your 'fabulous summer' plans* I talk about having a staycation in your home town. Well, let's get our home on board too and make it a peaceful and relaxing place to be in the summer, even if we are heading off to work five days a week.

When I think about having a second home as a weekend or vacation getaway, phrases come to mind and the kinds of things I think I'd do there are:

- It is easy to maintain.
- There are not too many possessions to care for.
- Any necessary housework is quick and easy to do.
- We only have a few clothes there, just what we need.
- There is a simple kitchen to make quick and delicious summer meals.
- We have space and time to nap, play, rest, and read.
- We get to really relax and 'be' with our loved ones whether it's a full family with children, just us, or with pets.
- There is lots of sunshine, open doors, and big windows.

Doesn't that just sound divine? It would be the kind of place you could go to and rejuvenate before coming back to daily life. But most of us don't have a second home, and even if we go on vacation, it is unlikely to be for the whole summer. So let's see how we can live like this every day at home.

Brainstorm for yourself what your ideal summer home would look like, how it would feel to be there, what kinds of things you would do while you're staying, and then see how you can more closely mesh this ideal into your everyday life.

Here are a few ideas to help you start making your home feel more summery inside and out.

1. **Open your windows** as much as possible. If it's very warm where you are, do it early in the morning before you switch the air conditioning on. Same if you go to work, open them early even if only for an hour or two.

2. Air and **pack away wintry items** such as throw rugs, big blankets and even some pillow covers. This seems so obvious, but I can't tell you how many times I have failed to notice a throw rug folded over the corner of the sofa when it's far past spring!

3. **Strip down your décor**. The cozy *hygge* look is great for when it's cooler, but in the heat of summer it feels beachy and summery to just have a few things out. Put items away and rotate them – they will seem fresh and new when you see them again, which is just an added bonus.

4. **Simplify your kitchen**. Throw out expired condiments and pantry items and make space for fresh summer salad vegetables and fruit. Clear off the kitchen counter and store everything but your most used items out of sight. If you have no room in your cabinets to do this have a twenty minute decluttering session and bring out small appliances or occasional dishes that you know you never use. Either donate them or store elsewhere for a limited

time to decide if you really do want them in your home.

5. Work out **a simple housework regime** so you can feel like you are on vacation. If possible, hire a house cleaner to come in and do the basics, even if it's just for the summer. Consider it part of your 'vacation at home' vibe. Put on a load of laundry as soon as the basket is full; it makes a huge difference to how relaxed and in control you will feel. The sight of an overflowing laundry basket is an instant puncture to your balloon of happiness!

6. Make everything easier on yourself by choosing to **simplify, declutter, and keep up to date**. Read decluttering inspiration such as Peter Walsh, Marie Kondo, Cassandra Aarssen and whoever else you can find. Watch decluttering shows on television. The Minimal Mom on YouTube has been a huge motivation to me. She is so down-to-earth and inspiring. Find someone who clicks with you and let them be your from-afar mentor.

7. If you have somewhere else to store clothes in your home, keep just **your idealistic summer capsule wardrobe** in your main closet. Imagine you have packed your suitcase to go on vacation and you're only taking your nicest and newest things. Wear those for

everyday! Obviously they have to be somewhat appropriate for the occasion, but if you're like me, you will want to keep the slightly fancier clothes for that mythical 'good enough' occasion, when the truth is, you can make a normal day a special occasion when you elevate how you dress.

8. When you go on a summer holiday, a big part of it is **choosing your reading material** – is it a stack of glossy magazines? A novel that is complete trash and oh-so-fun to read? Curate your summer reading and make a spot for it near where you relax.

9. Fill your fridge with your summer home staples. Stack containers filled with washed and prepped salad ingredients, fresh fruit salad and all the kinds of things you can picture yourself **dining on at a tropical resort**. My favourite vacation breakfast is fresh fruit, Greek yoghurt and sliced almonds as mentioned in *Chapter 8. Become a smoothie girl*. Whenever I have this at home it feels like I am on holiday. Clean out and stage your fridge so that it looks extra appealing.

These are just a few of my favourite ways to feel like I am living in my summer home, and I'm sure you will have thought of a few more while reading this chapter. I hope you enjoy staying at your vacation home this summer, and the best thing is that there is zero travel time and the cost is free!

Your Chic Summer tips:

- **Imagine your ideal summer home**, perhaps based on a place you have stayed at in the past, or from a television program or movie. Nancy Meyers movies always have great homes. Then, take note of all the little details you can borrow: blue and white striped pillows, check! Eating outside with a candle in a hurricane lamp, check! Reading a magazine with a cool drink, check!

- **Slip into a vacation state of mind** and look for how you can make everything *easier*. There is no need for meals that take ages to make, just grill something on the barbeque and bring out a salad you made earlier, or buy everything ready-made from the store. You are on *vacation*.

- **Do a little light decluttering** and organizing so you can feel like you are in a new place. Strip down and stage your home as if someone is renting it from you over the summer as a short-term Airbnb. The bonus is that this person is you, and you get to stay for nothing!

Chapter 13.
Staying chic in the heat

Aside from all the practical things we can do to have a wonderful summer in spite of the sometimes overwhelming heat and perhaps humidity too, we can get our mind in the right place. I always notice that when my mind is calm I am able to deal with so much more. And when I'm being negative and moany, even little upsets really rock my equilibrium, sometimes for several hours. What a waste of a day!

So with this in mind, I want to remind you (and myself) to **resist the urge to complain about the heat**. Zip your lips! Sometimes it is just habit, and we don't even realize we are moaning, yet again about how hot it is and how sticky we feel. *Yes, we all feel it, Fiona*, I imagine people around me thinking.

Instead, you can be the poised lady who exudes mystique, who, even though there are beads of moisture on her upper lip, smiles serenely and looks like she doesn't even notice how hot it is. She has more interesting things on her mind than complaining about the weather.

And the fabulous thing is, when you do this, the discomfort recedes. When you don't fight it in your mind and say it 'should' be different, you won't notice it as much. Telling yourself, 'This is only temporary' and then carrying on with what you were doing despite feeling a trickle run down the middle of your back will bring you a feeling of peace. Resisting it only makes it bigger in your mind.

And for some of us there can be hot flashes thrown in. That really adds to the mix! But again, when you resist them, they will bother you more. I know this from experience. And when you choose to accept that what is happening is just a part of life, the annoyance is lessened. Maybe you will take off a layer of clothing if you can, and then put it back on again later if you feel cool, or maybe you'll drink a glass of iced water.

But for me, I mostly just ride it out. After all, it's really only a few minutes at a time isn't it, even if sometimes you get a lot more episodes in one day than another!

Embrace the glow

Something I like to do which helps immensely when the weather is particularly humid, which I find unbearable like a lot of people, is to think about its main good point: humidity keeps the moisture levels in your skin high. So it's actually moisturizing your skin really well. Isn't that wonderful? Yes, you're still hot and sticky, but at least you are getting some benefit from it. That damp feeling you have is actually you, looking younger!

There are some things you can do though; here are my favourite tips for the hottest days:

- If you are at home, **dampen a face cloth** with cool water, wring it out and lay it over the back of your neck for a while. Perhaps even put it in the fridge and get it out periodically. An alternative to this is to take a cotton bandanna and twist it into a rope or fold into a ribbon and do the same as with the face flannel. You could even do this at work if the colour of the scarf doesn't look too different when wet.

- Keep a bottle of **refreshing fragrance** near you. I bought myself a bottle of 4711 – yes it is still around – which I remember from visiting my grandmother in the 1970s, and I keep this on my writing desk in the summer. It is very citrusy and refreshing to spritz on my wrists. It is zingy at the time, but doesn't last long, so it's a good office option.

- I also like to put any combo of **lemon, orange, mandarin or lime** essential oils in my oil diffuser which is a great alternative if you don't want to put perfume on your skin or are looking for something more natural. They have wellbeing benefits along with smelling good too. A quick online search showed that lemon oil can put you in a better mood, soothe anxiety and lift the spirits. Who knows if that is scientifically true or not, but I do know that I always feel good when I diffuse essential oils.

- **Evian mist in a can** is an old favourite that has been around since the 1980s it feels like. A quick spritz to your face from arm's length won't affect your makeup, and will give you a glorious fresh feeling. You don't even have to buy that exact can – any fine mist sprayer can be used. There are beautifully scented sprays available, I had a small rose water spray recently which is now used up, but it was so pretty to use. And currently I have a coconut scented Pure Fiji facial mist which is intended to be used as part of your regime when washing your face. But I have been using it to set my makeup (it looks so good when you do this as a final step, slightly dewy but not changed in any other way), and during the day when I think about it.

- Metal or plastic insulated cups/bottles with **ice or ice water** are a fabulous addition when it's hot. I bought two metal insulated bottles inexpensively. If I'm out for the day they stay cool in my car, so you could definitely do this for a long work day. I fill one to the top with ice and fill the rest of the space with water. And I half-fill the other with ice and then fill with water. I drink that one first, and then the second bottle after. At home, I have an insulated cup with a lid and straw, and this sits on my writing desk. Again, I fill it with ice and water and it feels *so good* to have that icy liquid go down! Using a straw means my sensitive teeth don't get zinged so much either.

I'm sure these aren't the only 'keep cool' tips around, they're just ones that I use regularly and that work for me. Ask others how they cope and try out any that appeal, and keep them in your chic toolbox for the hottest days.

Your Chic Summer tips:

- Take the phrase '**It's only temporary**' as your mantra this summer when you are tempted to complain about something related to the heat. Because it is! Focus on the good parts, get through the uncomfortable parts, and smooth out your experience to be enjoyable right through summer.

- Think about your skin when it's humid – your skin is being **moisturized for free**! How lucky are you!

- Use the **chic tools** listed in this chapter to try out a few new techniques. You will likely already have a facial mist in your bathroom cabinet, and a drink bottle in your kitchen. Perhaps you will make your own facial mist using half and half water and facial toner in a spray bottle. It feels good to use what you have!

Bonus Chapter.
From 'Thirty More Chic Days'

I wrote this chapter for my book *Thirty More Chic Days* which was released in 2018. You may already have this book, but I thought if you don't, it would be a fun addition as a bonus chapter, since the topic *is* the same. And if you do already own *Thirty More Chic Days*, please don't feel short-changed! Please consider this bonus chapter a refresher and reminder on living chicly in the summer.

And so, may I present to you Day 8 from *Thirty More Chic Days*, 'Be Chic in the Summer':

I have always found winter more of a chic challenge than summer, so much so that I wrote an entire book on how to survive the cold season. It's called 'How to be Chic in the Winter' and is still incredibly popular today; but I've had many ladies write to me and say, *When are you going to do 'How to be Chic in the*

Summer?' and saying how they found it difficult to stay chic when the weather was so hot.

It can take me a while to write a book, so I thought I would include a chapter in *Thirty More Chic Days* and share what has worked for me in the meantime. I don't remember summers being so challenging, but maybe I've had my rose-tinted sunglasses on, showing summers as being balmy and effortless, because this past summer I did not find it easy at all! Perhaps part of it for me is my changing hormones 'at a certain age'.

I am in my late forties and I realized that I definitely felt different. Firstly, my weight seemed to be creeping up even though I was not eating that differently. Secondly, my core body temperature felt higher; in addition, I would have times during the day when I felt even warmer, like I'd been lit up from the inside. Thirdly, if I exerted myself too much (or even if I hadn't), I'd have palpitations quite easily. I felt somewhat relieved when I found out these were all symptoms of changing hormones.

Aside from all that though, I could see that past summers being looked upon with fondness *were* me viewing them through a tinted filter. Looking at the upcoming summer filled me with mild anxiety about how I could keep my healthy meals on track when daylight savings promoted the 'vacation drinks and nibbles' feeling every night. What was I going to do with my hair when it was humid outside? And most importantly, what was I going to *wear* on the hottest days, so I could still feel my chicest self?

Curate your summer wardrobe

The clothing aspect is the first one to focus on, because if we want to feel like we haven't given up on life, having at least a small selection of nice outfits to feel good in is a must. At the beginning of the season I look through my last year's summer clothes and see what I want to keep and what is looking a bit past it.

Depending on the item, I will repurpose clothes that are not looking their pristine best to home lounge wear. I'm not talking about clothes that have rips or stains, just that they no longer look quite so 'new'. If there is something that is damaged and cannot be mended or cleaned, I will either cut it up for cleaning rags or throw it out.

It's also 'interesting' to see how items fit from last year. I try not to freak out about it too much if everything seems a little snugger than I remember; it's a good reminder that sugar *is not* my friend, it just pretends to be.

The way I decide whether I am going to put an item away until next year or donate it now, is by asking myself whether I am excited to see that item. Can I imagine myself wearing it and feeling sexy and fashionable? Or is the highest praise I can muster up, 'Well it's still in good condition...' You will know that feeling when you get out your next season's clothes and think, 'Yay! I forgot about this; I love it!' Or perhaps it's more along the lines of, 'Urgh; I put this away last summer thinking it would magically become more appealing'. Spoiler alert: those pieces never do.

With these items it can be hard to let them go because it seems wasteful, but when I do make the decision to donate it feels like a weight has been lifted.

I am suddenly more excited about my closet when I don't have to make the decision to avoid wearing that ever-so-slightly frumpy top again. And the ridiculous thing about my procrastination is that someone else might be thrilled with that top and it will look amazing on them. Win/win!

Choose your favourite silhouettes

From previous summers I have decided that I am a dress girl rather than a skirt and top girl when it's too hot to wear jeans (which are my staple for most of the year). I like dresses that are semi-tailored and knee-length or slightly above. Because I am short-waisted it is better for me to have no waistline on my dress.

Think back to outfits you have felt great in and look for more of those. Maybe it's three-quarter pants and a blouse in a soft fabric. Maybe it's floaty boho dresses. I think it's great that with the different seasons we can explore different sides of our own personal style.

Have a play around with the capsule wardrobe concept and design yourself a chic seasonal collection that you can mix and match (or just find half-a-dozen dresses you can rotate like I do!).

For me, I've found that well-made tee-shirt dresses can be worn with flip-flops or wedge heels. I bought three the same in black, red and navy/white stripes from Banana Republic four or five years ago and they've just about done their dash now. I got so much use from these dresses and I'm glad that I bought all three colours at once. The fabric is slightly thicker than normal tee-shirt material (double-faced jersey is the official term), so they were able to be worn to more places than a thin tee-shirt dress which really is only good for over your swimwear.

I've also enjoyed wearing soft denimy-chambray shift dresses the past few summers. They are easy to wash and give a quick press (if at all); I can still feel like 'me' in denim and they go with my shoes and accessories which suit my jeans look.

Plus, they're quite hard-wearing and not so easy to tear which is useful when our little rescue dogs get a bit over-excited. One of my favourite blush-pink tee-shirts had a tiny hole plucked in the front from an enthusiastic doggy claw which was very upsetting!

Fun tip: Look at movies or television programs set in the summer to see how the actresses dress. A costume designer's job is to put together a wardrobe to reflect a character's personality, so if you like one outfit they are wearing, it's likely you will gain some new ideas from other outfits in the same movie.

Think 'cooling beauty'

I have wavy hair that frizzes in humid weather, and what I have found is good for hot, sticky days is to wash my hair and slick it back into a low bun like a ballet dancer would. To look polished, I like to roll a cotton scarf into a long ribbon and wind that around my bun a few times, finishing with a tiny knot.

Not only do I look (and feel) pulled together, but my hair being damp starts my day off on a cool note. I use a leave-in conditioning treatment, mousse or gel, so when I brush my hair out that night it feels silky and healthy.

If we have a day when it is not so humid and I'm at home, I like to let my hair dry naturally in waves. Later on, I might blow-dry around my hairline with a brush to finish off the look.

I also like to play around with other hairstyles that keep my hair off my neck such as stylish ponytails or experimenting with French braids (practice makes perfect!)

With makeup, I have found Estée Lauder's Double Wear foundation excellent on hot days. I let my SPF moisturizer soak in while I have breakfast, then blot with a tissue to remove perspiration from my skin (it's usually on my nose and upper lip when the weather is warm!). I then apply it with a sponge.

I have changed from using my fingers or a foundation brush to a Beauty Blender sponge and love it. I started out with a proper Beauty Blender and after a while when it no longer cleaned up as well, I tried a $4 cheapie which is just as good. I'm glad I tried both price options otherwise I'd always have wondered. Sometimes cheaper versions of an item work fine, and sometimes they don't.

When it comes to body-care, I moisturize all over every day as I do in the winter, but in summer I add a gradual tanner to my beauty regime. I also wear SPF 15 moisturizer on my décolletage, because I can go quite pink there. I bought myself an inexpensive epilator which I use on my legs to free me from shaving them. Every so often I will shave my legs in between epilations because I find this helps exfoliate my skin and prevent ingrown hairs.

Eating well in the heat

The one saving grace of summer is that salads are more appealing than in the winter, when I crave stodgy, warm, comforting food. My top tip for eating healthy in the summer is to *prepare ingredients ahead of time.*

Having a vegetable chiller full of bell peppers, carrots, lettuce and other salad ingredients is great, but then you still have to wash and slice them. What I do now is have a chop-a-thon a few times a week where I fill GladWare or Tupperware containers with all manner of jewel-toned goodness. You could mix salad ingredients together so that you have one big container to ladle a portion into a bowl at lunchtime, or be like me and have smaller individual containers of ingredients. Doing it this way appeals; it feels like I am at a gourmet salad bar putting my lunch together.

I don't buy salads often, but when I do they always help me like salads more as well as give me new combinations to try. When I worked next-door to a Subway, I was inspired to recreate my own version of their salad at home. I'd have fresh vegetable ingredients ready to go, adding a topping of shredded cheese to my chopped cold roast chicken. I also invested in a lidded salad container to eat from, so I could pour my salad dressing on at the end and give the whole thing a good shake to mix everything together.

Plus, having a couple of lidded salad containers meant I could pre-make a few salads and then add the dressing right before I ate. The less barriers to eating healthy, the better.

But what about after work, when you get the vacation feeling as you arrive home in the blazing sunshine? I say take the vacation feeling all the way and pretend you aren't at home having to go to work the next day. Go for a stroll around the neighbourhood before dinner, read a book for a little while, then cook a tiny and exquisite steak on the barbeque to serve with green beans and new potatoes.

If you do have to do a load of laundry, do it after dinner while you are organising your clothes for the next day. I don't always set out my outfits the night before, but when I do it's fun to add the extra accessories or wear something a bit better than I normally might. Having more fun with my clothing choices brings about a vacation feeling for me as well.

Transport yourself to the South of France (or wherever that dream place is for you)

When I think about my summer successes, it's because I've prepared ahead of time. I find outfits that are comfortable and attractive to wear and I replicate them. I imagine what a rich and glamorous lady might eat on her yacht and I make that for lunch or dinner. I slick my hair back and dust a light coating of bronzer on my cheekbones, temples and the tip of my nose like I'm heading to downtown St Tropez to stroll around, browse the shops and maybe grab a coffee in a café.

I am still the Paris girl of my dreams; the only difference is that she has caught the high-speed train down to the South of France for her summer vacation! I dress and act accordingly, even though I am still living my normal life in my everyday surroundings in Hawke's Bay, New Zealand. *Why not?* I say.

Thirty Chic Days inspirational ideas:

Come up with a theme for your summer. As I have shared, I love the thought of my inner Paris girl heading off to the South of France for her summer season. Maybe yours is the NYC girl going to the Hamptons or your inner Londoner jetting to Spain.

Whatever the inspiration is for you, **let your inner stylista and happy girl guide you** through a fun and glamorous summer. Eat the juicy fresh foods she nudges you to prepare, enjoy your curated closet and have fun trying out summer hairstyles.

At the beginning of the hot season, **decide that this is going to be your best summer yet**, and it will be!

50 Ways to be Chic in the Summer

We have come to the end! Thank you so much for reading *How to be Chic in the Summer*. I am thrilled to be here with you, creating your wonderful summer season. If you have read any of my books before, you will know I love an inspiring and uplifting *list of goodness* to finish off. There is just something about a list that is so delightfully motivating, don't you find?

So lets dive into the cool water of our ideal summer, and soak languidly in fifty ways to be chic when it's hot outside. Follow me!

1. **Be a summer diva**. Know you are going to look and feel fabulous this summer, and it all starts with claiming being *queen*!

2. **Start your 'chic summer' journal** or computer document, and write down ideas to try, inspiration you create for yourself, outfit combos and more. Keep all your inspiration in one place; not only will it be fun to create now, but you'll benefit from it in summers to come as well.

3. Keep your 'chic summer' plans **in your secret garden**. Don't blab about them to others. They are just for you.

4. Make a **list of chic summer plans** and put them in a place you can see them. Don't let another summer go by without ticking some of them off.

5. Make a **summer book list** for yourself and enjoy the downtime. Even if you're not sitting poolside at a luxury resort you can still set up a little area at home.

6. **Invite people around** and create a movie-worthy simple gathering. In my mind I imagine us all sitting outside at night laughing and chatting, there are LED candles on the table and everyone has enjoyed their casual meal. Make your vision happen, and work out how to make it easy on yourself too – serve a simple menu and have fun.

7. Do **jobs early in the day**. Even if it seems crazy early, like prepping salad before breakfast. You will be so glad of that bowl of deliciousness in the fridge come dinner time when you have no oomph left.

8. **Make things easy on yourself**. Simplify your home, your schedule, your closet... Now is not the time for complicated. Even if you're at work and not on vacation, you can still enjoy a vacation feeling by simplifying down to the basics.

9. Keep **up to date with your chores** so you don't have things hanging over you. Little and often is the key! Do things when you see them, and do them as quick as you can.

10. **Curate your chic summer look**. Play around in your wardrobe and pull together a 21-piece collection of clothes that you would happily wear *today*. Give yourself fifteen minutes to do this and you will amaze yourself with how good the results are.

11. Search **Pinterest for new ideas** and see if you can use your clothes in different combinations.

12. Use **accessories in summer ways** – a folded scarf as a headband, or tie it around your ponytail or handbag strap.

13. **Wear a cocktail ring** instead of a necklace when it's hot. There are tons of inexpensive and stylish options for a pop of wow-factor to finish off your look.

14. Design yourself a summer look that **borrows from your winter style** if you are more of a cool weather lady. Or, go the complete opposite to your winter style and be a bi-style dresser. It's like being bi-coastal but with less travel!

15. Don't beat yourself up if you have put on weight over winter. Be positive, work with what you have, and **focus on your healthy lifestyle** as well as being *totally fabulous*.

16. Spend a few hours **trying on dresses** in different styles. Go by yourself and make it a goal to get in and out of stores as quickly as possible. If the dress looks terrible, it's the dress and not you. Put it back and try on the next one.

17. Glam up with **a pair of summery wedge sandals** that you find comfortable to walk in.

18. Self-tan every day or every second day and then maintain, alternating tanning with moisturizing. **Use gradual tanner** for easier application and a better result.

19. Wear **colours that make you feel happy**. If it's black in the summer, fab. If it's candy pink,

cool. Choose what rings *your* bell regardless of what people say is appropriate or in vogue.

20. **Be your own personal stylist** – be both parts: you and her! Go through your closet together and *make magic*.

21. Find a character to channel and **be your muse this summer** – she might be someone you know, a book character, or from a movie or television series. It doesn't matter who you choose, just *how she makes you feel*: empowered, fabulous, like your best self, and ready to be a savvy fashionista.

22. Decide to be **confident in everything you do**. Try it on and see how it feels. Having confidence is one of the best things you can do to become more attractive and *you can choose it for yourself*. Decide to be the most confident person you know. Be *that girl*.

23. Find **your best summer hair do** and rock it. Practice, research, people-watch. Put a little time and effort in – it always comes back to this for me. I can be lazy with many things, but with my hair it shows!

24. **Try dry shampoo** if you haven't already. I prefer 'clean' feeling not volumizing dry shampoos. You may be different.

25. **Define your eyes** so even if your makeup starts to disappear throughout the day, you will still look made up.

26. Wear **SPF on your decolletage** as well as your face, every single day.

27. **Pamper your feet** with a pumice stone a few times a week and massage them with cream morning and night.

28. Have **a professional pedicure** at the beginning of summer and see how nice your brightly painted toes look.

29. Find a **healthy, delicious and easy breakfast** that you *adore*, like my smoothies are for me.

30. **Add something fresh** to your current meals: sliced fruit, or a side salad.

31. **Reframe salads** from boring **to glamorous**. Be that Beverly Hills lady who has a big salad and sparkling water for lunch. Remember to add protein so you stay full until dinner.

32. Add the fun, slightly less healthy toppings to salads to **make them more appealing**. For me, grated Parmesan cheese, and a creamy Caesar dressing.

33. **Grow your own herbs** and maybe some tomatoes too. Plant tomatoes and other summer vegetables such as cucumber in May for the Northern Hemisphere and November in the Southern Hemisphere.

34. Be **a summer slow-cooker girl** and make life easier as well as keeping your kitchen cool.

35. **Dine like a chic lady** and drink like one too. Sip, don't chug your chilled beverage (I need reminding of this sometimes!)

36. Place **a glass of water** next to your wine glass. You will find that you need to refill your water glass often because you drink from it without noticing.

37. **Dress your table**, even if it's 'just' for the family on a normal night and even if it's just some pretty summery napkins rather than paper towels.

38. Design **your summer drinks menu** and include plenty of alcohol-free choices to either replace or supplement your wine or cocktail options.

39. Makeover your home to be **your summer home**. A few changed décor items, putting heavier fabrics away and giving everything a

good clean and tidy will have you feeling like you've moved into a luxury Airbnb.

40. Find mentors (décor books, decluttering experts, or organizing shows) who help you **streamline your home** for summer and beyond.

41. If you have the space, put all your winter clothes in a different closet and keep just **your summer collection in your main closet**. Hang everything up too, even tee-shirts.

42. Dine like you imagine you would at **a luxury health resort**. Picture an abundant buffet there: what would you like for dinner?

43. Choose to be in **a vacation state of mind** as much as possible. It will make everything feel more relaxed and easier. You can still get everything done that needs to get done. Choose a calm, peaceful and breezy feeling in your mind instead of hurry, rush and stress.

44. **Do some summer decluttering**. Take a look around and see what no longer fits the beautiful vision you have for your life and gift those items to a charity who could benefit.

45. **Surround yourself with citrus**: lemon slices in your water, fresh orange pieces in a fruit salad, lemon verbena French soap, or lime

essential oil in your diffuser or dropped onto a cotton ball to tuck away in a drawer.

46. Refresh your face with a light misting of Evian or any other water spray. Take a moment to **breathe deep and relax your shoulders** as you spritz.

47. Keep a **light, bright fragrance** on your desk and use it as a form of aromatherapy. I like to apply to my wrists before bed as well, for a dreamy way to drift off to sleep.

48. **Sip iced water** and feel your internal temperature instantly cool. Use a straw if you have sensitive teeth like me.

49. **Never complain about the heat**. Being hot in summer is just a given. Focusing on it will not help you feel cooler, but instead do the opposite. Just ignore it as much as you can.

50. **Practice your positive mindset**. Tell yourself this is going to be your best summer yet, and it will be!

This list is just a starting point for you; now you get to add to the ideas, use any of mine that appeal, and create your most wonderful summer, as big and powerful or small and peaceful as you like. You get to choose. And you get to change your mind at any moment too. It's all your creation.

I wish you a happy and fun summer season and truly hope the ideas in this book will make a difference for you. It's my intention with all of my books that you, the reader, receives far more in value than the purchase price. Ten times if not one hundred times more value.

Sometimes it only takes one idea to shift you completely, and others it is a slow progression of mindset shifts and one day you realize that, hey, you actually feel really sunny and bright most of the time.

That's how I feel most days, and it's fabulous. I hope you'll join me in the shimmery dreamworld that is your fabulously chic summer. I'll see you on the beach in our fancy coverups, umbrella drink in one hand and airport novel in the other. Cheers to us!

Fiona

A note from the author

Thank you for reading *How to be Chic in the Summer*! My sincere wish is that this book has left you in a sunny and optimistic frame of mind.

If you enjoyed *How to be Chic in the Summer*, I would be so grateful for a review on Amazon, even if it's only a few words. Reviews are very important to authors! It's how other readers find our books. I read all reviews of my books to get your feedback, and hope to make my future books better by doing this.

Thank you in advance if you are happy to leave a review, and I wish all the best for your most fabulous summer yet!

About the author

Fiona Ferris is passionate about the topic of living well, in particular that a simple and beautiful life can be achieved without spending a lot of money.

Her books are published in five languages currently: English, Spanish, Russian, Lithuanian and Vietnamese. She also runs an online home study program for aspiring non-fiction authors.

Fiona lives in the beautiful and sunny wine region of Hawke's Bay, New Zealand, with her husband, Paul, their rescue cats Jessica and Nina and rescue dogs Daphne and Chloe.

You can find Fiona's other books at:
amazon.com/author/fionaferris
payhip.com/fionaferris

You can connect with Fiona at:
howtobechic.com
fionaferris.com
instagram.com/fionaferrisnz
facebook.com/fionaferrisauthor
twitter.com/fiona_ferris
youtube.com/fionaferris

Book Bonuses

http://bit.ly/ThirtyChicDaysBookBonuses

Type in the link above to receive your free special bonuses.

'21 ways to be chic' is a fun list of chic living reminders, with an MP3 recording to accompany it so you can listen on the go as well.

Excerpts from Fiona's books in PDF format.

You will also **receive a subscription** to Fiona's blog *'How to be Chic'*, for inspiration on living a simple, beautiful and successful life.

Printed in Germany
by Amazon Distribution
GmbH, Leipzig